THE
BAR MITZVAH
MOTHER'S MANUAL

THE
BAR MITZVAH
MOTHER'S
MANUAL

Alice Keidan Lanckton

HIPPOCRENE BOOKS

New York   1986

For information, address: Hippocrene Books, Inc.
171 Madison Avenue, New York, NY   10016

ISBN 0-87052-283-3

Printed in the United States of America

Contents

For Van

Acknowledgments

THANKS first and most to my husband, Van, who always took this project seriously and humorously. His encouragement, help, and kidding around were as necessary to me as an author as they are to me in everything else

I thank my son Ben for giving us all the great pleasure of being a Bar Mitzvah family and for teaching us more about meaningful Judaism.

My son Sam has helped me keep my ideas in perspective with his keen writer's sense, his wise advice, and his smart remarks. He has also been my calm and constant on-the-premises computer consultant.

Meg McCann loaned me her very own computer for a whole summer so that this manuscript could be completed before school began. She also let me call her seventeen times a day until the computer became Alice-friendly.

Ruth Vignati kept this book a secret for years, all the while listening sympathetically to progress reports.

Diane Fulman encouraged me and advised me on the manuscript.

Marsha Slotnick, in a way, gave me my start in the whole business: she told me how she had prepared for Nancy's Bat Mitzvah celebration.

Marcy Greenfield, Flo Ziffer, Herb Greenberg, and Sue Ebert contributed significantly to my education about special needs Bar and Bat Mitzvah.

Sincere thanks to my very dear family and to all these good friends and the many others who have talked and listened Bar Mitzvah with me for years.

It is with love, admiration, and gratitude that I dedicate this book to my husband, Van.

Alice Keidan Lanckton

A Note on Gender

THROUGHOUT this book I refer mostly to the "Bar" Mitzvah and the "Bar" Mitzvah mother, father, boy, family. This usage, rather than "Bar or Bat" Mitzvah, is not because I am sexist. (I probably am, somewhat, although my husband did type most of this manuscript.)

More to the point, my children are boys, and so I talk most authentically about Bar rather than Bat Mitzvah. It seems awkward for me to say "Bar or Bat" every time I mention them (it). So, with apologies to the mothers of girls, I proceed. Please know that I mean both when I say one. And you have my special sympathy, since I remember too well what I was like when I was thirteen.

Chapter one

What's a nice young woman like me doing at her roommate's son's Bar Mitzvah?

A BAR MITZVAH used to be a simple, infrequent event. It happened to a neighbor's son or a cousin. It required only some calls to find a babysitter and a trip to the bookstore for a copy of *Bartlett's Familiar Quotations,* my standard gift.

However, the frequency of Bar Mitzvahs began to increase. Then the whole family was invited down to Connecticut for my college roommate's son's Bar Mitzvah. And I realized that I had known the young man of the hour for all his thirteen years and was, in fact, quite moved that he had come so far. And, by the way, he looked not so much older than our eleven-year-old son, Ben.

This was getting serious; it was going to happen in our family, too. Anxiety immediately set in.

Sharon's son chanted his Torah portion with great confidence.

Would our son do the same? Sharon's son also had some rather interesting things to say about Isaiah. Would our religious school cover the prophets? Sharon used to be interested only in philosophy and Joseph Conrad. How had she learned to arrange what my mother would have called "such a lovely luncheon"?

And, more important, what would become of me, a person who thought she was interested in only the really significant things in life? Here I was, noticing that navy tablecloths look good with burnt orange napkins but that the flowers are too tall to talk over.

It seemed to me that I had just stopped buying disposable diapers. How could I be a Bar Mitzvah mother already? Those are real big-time women who wear hats. They talk to caterers, select colors, and have to stand up in front of the whole congregation. I am a perfectly nice young mother with a new part-time job three and a half days a week. I am much too young, sensible, and busy to become some kind of Philip Roth caricature. Whatever is this Bar Mitzvah going to mean for me?

It was all so remote and threatening before our son Ben's Bar Mitzvah. However, I am pleased to report that the reality turned out to be not only a wonderful event but also an important, interesting process for all of us, a coming of age for the whole family.

Sure it was a million phone calls and details and last-minute changes, but it was a real education for us, as it can be for you.

Just as we did, you'll be able to discover more exactly what Judaism can mean for your family. You'll confront issues in parenting a teenager while you also must act as a mature child to older parents. You'll find you have skills you didn't know you had as a social planner and hostess.

You'll do all this best if you keep remembering that planning for a Bar Mitzvah is a *good* problem. Some of the problems we have to solve are very tough, like illness or unemployment. Some are irritating, like getting the washer fixed. Some are repetitious and ornery, like getting the kids to pick up their underwear and practice the clarinet.

What's a nice young woman doing here?

But planning a Bar Mitzvah service and celebration? That's a good problem to solve and an interesting rite of passage for you as well. However, there's no reason for you to do it alone. You ought to benefit from the experience of others who have been through it before. So, turn the page.

Chapter two

Networking: What did she do for her Bar Mitzvah?

WHEN OUR SON Ben was still the Bar Mitzvah irrelevant age of six, I stood in line at the market behind a woman who had, apparently, masterminded her son's recent Bar Mitzvah. "I did the whole thing myself," she told the entire express line. *Even the Torah reading?* I wondered meanly. How could she be so foolish, acting as if it were her Bar Mitzvah because she did a lot of cooking and planning?

She was wrong on more counts than I knew then; but I've learned she was a tiny bit right as well. You certainly won't have to read the Torah or need to put on a tallit. However, a Bar Mitzvah mother does turn out to have many important responsibilities, experiences, and feelings.

You will be instrumental in planning a service and celebration that you and your family will find meaningful and will enjoy.

17

You'll have a better time of it, though, if you put to one side how much credit you'll get for doing it singlehandedly.

Ask anyone who can help. As the *shtetl* mama tells her son who is leaving for America and unsure how he'll find his way, "You have a mouth. Open it."

Maybe you thought it terrific when Harriet's son announced at his Bar Mitzvah that he had adopted as a twin for the occasion a thirteen-year-old Soviet Jewish boy who was not allowed to celebrate his Bar Mitzvah. So Harriet's son was celebrating his twin's Bar Mitzvah for him. If you'd like your son to have a similar "twin," ask the rabbi or the educational director or call the Jewish Community Council. And, of course, ask for your son's approval at being twinned.

Perhaps you found it meaningful that a Torah was physically handed down from grandmother to mother to daughter at a Bat Mitzvah you went to in Cleveland. Consult your rabbi or ritual committee and see whether your family can do the same.

Don't hesitate to ask the experts at your temple for suggestions. The principal of the school, the executive director, of course the rabbi, and his secretary have the advantage of knowing the full range of what people at your temple have done. These folks are used to being consulted, and they often enjoy being asked.

Don't feel it's too early to consult with them if some question is bothering you, even quite far in advance. They will give you the basic requirements for the service and tell you what temple policies might affect your celebration. They have also learned from experience how families cope with delicate situations, like divorced Bar Mitzvah parents, and frustrating ones, like snowstorms.

You may well find that your temple gives classes for pre-Bar Mitzvah parents to acquaint them with the background of the event and current practice at that temple. Students are included in many such classes. You will want to take advantage of these.

Get advice about the celebration, too. If you liked the little mushroom crepes at your niece's Bat Mitzvah, call your sister-in-law. Even if she's not your best friend, she'll be pleased that you remember her party so fondly. It will give her a chance to talk about it again and renew the pleasure of the day. The same is true for whomever you call about invitations, music, flowers, and where your relatives ought to stay.

You can even call to investigate parties you've only heard about. I know I was delighted when a woman called whom I hadn't seen since my Bar Mitzvah's nursery school days. She had heard that our musicians were great and wanted their number. There's no reason you can't make someone feel good for being an expert and, in the process, make it easier on yourself to find flowers, get a hat, or make friends with the temple custodian.

You know other experts, too. Any friends who have recently given a large party—graduation, engagement, birthday celebration—will have something to teach you. Ask them what turned out best and what pitfalls to watch for.

But, before you reach for the phone, a few words about how this whole Bar Mitzvah came to be.

Chapter three

Bar Mitzvah history: How did we get from Canaan to the caterer's?

"BLESSED BE HE who has relieved me from the responsibility for this child." This is a father's prayer from midrashic literature of the eighth century.* With this blessing the father announced that his child was now held accountable for his own actions. This prayer is the oldest Jewish coming-of-age ritual.

The specific ages of thirteen for boys and twelve for girls were established as legal Jewish adulthood by the sixth century. The Talmud, compiled at this time, makes it clear that at these ages Jews became subject to the commandments. From then on a Jew was responsible for his own promises, could be a member of a minyan (if a man), and should fast on Yom Kippur. The title

*This prayer is still the traditional father's blessing at modern Orthodox Bar Mitzvahs.

bestowed on the young man who came of age was "son [Bar] of the commandment [Mitzvah]."

By the fourteenth century in Europe, the boy celebrated his Bar Mitzvah with his first participation in the reading of the Torah portion at regular religious services.

The Torah portion merits explanation. The Torah consists of the five books of Moses. These trace the story of the beginnings of man and concentrate on the Exodus of the Jews from slavery in Egypt, their journey to the promised land of Israel, and the laws they received from God. To this day, the Torah is written by hand on a scroll.

Each congregation uses its own formula to determine which portion from the Torah will be read each week. It is traditional to read the scroll in sequence, ending and beginning again on the holiday of Simchat Torah in the fall. Some congregations use a three-year cycle instead of a one-year cycle. Many Reform congregations use most of the traditional sequence but leave out passages they find irrelevant to modern life.

Anyone who has the honor of reciting blessings over the Torah portion is said to be "called up" to the Torah. The Hebrew word "aliyah," or "going up," is the name for this honor. This Hebrew word is also used for the act of moving to Israel, since Israel is considered holier than all other places.

It remained true in the Middle Ages as it does today that all you must really do to become Bar Mitzvah is attain the age of thirteen. But the traditional ceremony in which the child gave evidence of his adult responsibility began to develop from this honor or aliyah of his first participation in the Torah service.

To demonstrate his ability as a man in the Jewish community, the Bar Mitzvah would read the blessings before and after one part of the day's Torah reading. He would also probably chant some of the Torah itself. The concluding part of the Torah portion, called the maftir, became the customary Bar Mitzvah portion.

The haftarah, which we tend to associate with Bar Mitzvah, is usually a selection from the writings of the Prophets. It always has some relationship to the Torah portion. The haftarah was added to the service when, in hostile countries, Jews were forbidden to read the Torah. They then read instead another holy book which put them in mind of the proper Torah reading for the day. It used to be the custom that younger children would read the day's haftarah; medieval synagogues always had stepstools around for them. However, this honored reading has come to belong to the Bar Mitzvah.

Sometime in the late Middle Ages the adult community decided to make the Bar Mitzvah the opportunity for the boy to discuss the sacred words as well as reading them. Thus was born the tradition of a lecture by the boy about the section of the Torah he read. In his lecture he would demonstrate his ability to understand the Torah interpretation he had studied in the Talmud, the famous compilation of commentary on the Torah.

Most often this lecture would take place at the boy's home on Shabbat afternoon after the services. All the learned men of the community would be invited. Of course, the proud mama would celebrate the occasion with something delicious for all to eat. This is probably the origin of the festive meal, called in Hebrew the "seudat mitzvah," the commanded banquet. A seudat mitzvah was already traditional for centuries before this as a celebration of the brit (circumcision) of an infant boy and for a wedding.

Though we tend to associate Bar Mitzvah with the ceremonies and celebrations of one special Shabbat, Bar Mitzvah continues to identify the time when a young man assumes all Jewish adult responsibilities (mitzvot) on an ongoing basis. As a practical matter, this commonly means that the young man begins to observe seriously those mitzvot that his father observes.

One very important sign of adult Jewish manhood is the wearing of tefillin, the cubical leather containers with attached leather thongs. These are worn by observant Jews during daily morning prayers, except on Shabbat, and contain four important biblical passages. Observant Jews begin to wear these at Bar Mitzvah, sometimes a bit before. You would, however, be unlikely to see them at a Bar Mitzvah ceremony since Bar Mitzvahs are usually celebrated on Shabbat when tefillin are not worn (though Bar Mitzvahs can also occur on Mondays and Thursdays).

Special ceremonies and customs have been added at the time of Bar Mitzvah at different times in Jewish history. The *conversos* ("marranos")* in Spain during the Inquisition had to keep their Judaism a secret. They pretended to embrace Christianity to save their lives and couldn't risk letting their children know that they were Jewish since the children might unwittingly give away the secret. So Bar Mitzvah, the age that bridges the time between childhood and adulthood, was chosen as the time for this important disclosure of the family's true identity. Though there was probably no Torah blessing—and, in fact, nothing as obvious and dangerous a sign of Judaism as a religous service—the Spanish Bar Mitzvah served as a dramatic demarcation point between innocent childhood and a dangerous, but precious, adult identity.

On a much lighter note . . . in eighteenth-century Italy, it was customary to have a poem composed in honor of a young man's Bar Mitzvah, and the custom spread to Holland and then to England. In the same century in Germany the rabbis had to enact a law to prohibit Bar Mitzvah boys from wearing wigs, which was a fashionable practice at the time for adults. Such a law suggests that boys (or their parents) wanted this mantle of adulthood worn for the coming-of-age ceremony. Why a law against it unless it was being done?

The Bat Mitzvah was a major new development in the twentieth century. Rabbi Mordecai Kaplan, founder of the Reconstructionist Movement, believed in a traditional Judaism which was nonetheless open to change so that the modern Jew could derive full satisfaction from his association with the Jewish people. Equality of the sexes was essential in this view. Consequently, Rabbi Kaplan prevailed on his somewhat reluctant twelve-year-old daughter,

---

Marranos means "swine" in Spanish. This derogatory term was used by the Christians to describe Jews converted to Christianity and suspected of secretly remaining Jewish. I use the less common, but more impartial, term *conversos*.

Judith, to celebrate the first Bat Mitzvah in America on May 5, 1922.

Invitations were sent out weeks in advance, but Rabbi Kaplan decided on the protocol for the new ceremony only the evening before, as he and Judith were going over the blessings. The next morning, as Judith recalls it,

> we all went together, Father, Mother, disapproving Grandmothers, my three little sisters and I. . . The first part of my own ordeal was to sit in that front room among the men, away from the cozy protection of mother and sisters.
>
> . . . Father was called up for the honor of reading the *Maftir*. . . . When he finished the *Haftorah* . . . I was signaled to a place below the *bimah* at a very respectable distance from the Scroll of the Torah which had already been rolled up and garbed in its mantle. I pronounced the first blessing, and from my own *Chumash* [Five Books of Moses] read the selection which Father had chosen for me, continued with the reading of the English translation and concluded with the closing *berachah* (blessing). That was it. The scroll was returned to the Ark with song and procession, and the service was resumed. No thunder sounded, no lightning struck. The institution of *Bat Mitzvah* had been born without incident, and the rest of the day was all rejoicing.*

Reform Judaism in the early twentieth century had abandoned the Bar Mitzvah ceremony. It had been eliminated because thirteen was considered too young for a modern Jew to come of age. Reform Jews had instead turned to the Confirmation service. Modeled on the Lutheran Confirmation ceremony, the Reform Jewish Confirmation was (and still is) held at the significantly more mature age of sixteen.

When Reform Jews resumed Bar Mitzvah ceremonies in the 1940s, they made good on their support for equality of the sexes and borrowed the Reconstructionist Bat Mitzvah as well. Gradu-

*Judith Kaplan Eisenstein, "No thunder sounded, no lightning struck," in Azriel Eisenberg, ed., *Eyewitnesses to American Jewish History, Part 4: The American Jew 1915–1969* (New York: Union of American Hebrew Congregations, 1982), pp. 31–32.

ally this practice has spread to many Conservative congregations and some Orthodox as well.

The major difference between Bar Mitzvah and Bat Mitzvah is that the girl in Judaism is considered mature at the age of twelve. Consequently, she is automatically Bat Mitzvah on her twelfth birthday. The ceremony, which can take place anytime after that, is often similar to whatever ceremony Bar Mitzvah requires at her temple. The education required of a Bat Mitzvah is also the same as that required of a Bar Mitzvah.

But, after all this history, you ask, what *is* standard these days for Bar and Bat Mitzvah ceremonies? I was just getting to that.

Chapter four

Current Bar and Bat Mitzvah practice:
Two Jews, three opinions

AS SOON AS I tell you that there are certain basic similarities in American Bar and Bat Mitzvah practice these days, you are bound to tell me that your sister's congregation in California never does any of those things and instead requires that the youngster demonstrate computer literacy and know his first and middle Hebrew names. However, except for your sister's congregation, there are usually some basic common components to the Jewish coming-of-age ceremony.

As described in the last chapter, an American Bar Mitzvah usually recites blessings over the Torah portion, reads from the Torah or haftarah, and gives some kind of speech.

But almost every congregation (even your sister's) is sensitive to the abilities of the child. An especially enthusiastic and able Bar Mitzvah may be encouraged to perform more than the traditional elements; some lead the whole service. Modifying the requirements for special needs of the child is discussed at length in chapter six. In chapter five ("Where do we belong?") I also discuss different temple and non-temple settings and ceremonies for Bar and Bat Mitzvahs.

The family of the Bar Mitzvah is usually honored during the temple service. In Orthodox congregations the male relatives and friends (who are over Bar Mitzvah age) are honored with aliyot. In non-Orthodox congregations, male and female relatives and friends can be so honored. They pronounce blessings, lead part of the services, give a commentary on the Torah reading, open the ark, or lift the Torah. The nonverbal aliyot provide a fine opportunity to honor someone who, though Jewish, is unable or diffident about reading Hebrew.

In addition to these ceremonies, the rabbi usually speaks to the Bar Mitzvah about his future as a Jewish adult. The father's prayer (described in chapter three) is usually said quietly at Orthodox Bar Mitzvahs. And in non-Orthodox congregations, both parents often recite the She-Heheyanu, a joyous expression of thanksgiving for a happy or new occasion. Often there is also the ancient three-part priestly blessing recited for the child by his parents or the rabbi.

At the religious ceremony the rabbi or an officer of the congregation usually presents a congregational gift. Some give a book of the Torah; some give a Kiddush cup for a Bar Mitzvah and candlesticks for a Bat Mitzvah. Some also give a certificate of Bar Mitzvah. (At the rehearsal they'll teach your youngster how to juggle the gifts while he's shaking hands with the rabbi.)

If the Torah is going to be read at the service, the Bar Mitzvah usually takes place on a Monday, Thursday, or Saturday. Most Bar Mitzvah ceremonies take place during the Saturday morning service, but it is also traditional to read the Torah and celebrate a Bar Mitzvah at a Monday or Thursday morning service or at the Saturday afternoon service.

The Shabbat afternoon service is concluded with the beautiful Havdalah ceremony. Havdalah is the separation of the Shabbat from the week. The brief and charming Havdalah ceremony includes the lighting of a long, braided candle and blessings over wine and a fragrant spice box.

So, traditionally Bar Mitzvahs can take place on Saturday morning or afternoon and on Monday and Thursday mornings. The Torah is also read on Rosh Hodesh, the first day of each Jewish month, which means that you have an added opportunity for the choice of a Bar Mitzvah date.

Then, there are the new nontraditional traditions. Some non-Orthodox congregations observe Bar or Bat Mitzvah ceremonies on Friday nights. Blessings are pronounced, passages from the Torah and haftarah are read, and the rabbi speaks to the young adult, all in the context of a Shabbat evening service. Bar Mitzvah mothers often receive the honor of lighting the Shabbat candles at such a service.

Some Orthodox congregations are not comfortable with women participating exactly as men do in the service. They find an acceptable compromise in celebrating the young woman's coming of age at home with a religious service which includes a Torah reading. Because of her family's strict adherence to Orthodox tradition, one young student of mine celebrated her Bat Mitzvah at home at a service attended only by women. (The men joined them for the festivities.)

In the past years other meaningful, imaginative additions have been made to the Bar Mitzvah. As mentioned earlier, it has become popular to "twin" an American Bar or Bat Mitzvah with a Soviet Jewish child who is not permitted to celebrate this occasion in the Soviet Union. Announcement of the twinning is made at the service, and the American child is given a certificate to keep for the Russian child until he can emigrate to freedom. The American child writes to the Soviet child, and some American families include both names on the invitations. (The appendix will help you find out how to twin and how to find a printer familiar with such invitations.)

Before a youngster assumes the responsibility of a Bar or Bat Mitzvah, some temples involve him in a study of the meaning of mitzvot (plural of mitzvah, or commandment). At our temple this was called the "Lamedvavnik" program.* The Hebrew letters *lamed* and *vav* are used together to represent the number 36; there is a talmudic tradition that the world goes on because of the righteous behavior of 36 righteous individuals. There are always 36, and there always have been 36. The moment one dies, another is born. So the Bar Mitzvah students emulate these 36 and set about doing 36 mitzvot in the months before their coming of age. Each week the rabbi and the students study the meaning of some of the different mitzvot, both ritual and intellectual as well as those relating to human relationships. The rabbi gives the students a list of many, and they select the 36 they want to do. My son Ben got credit for everything—from celebrating Havdalah to helping friends move to a new house.

Rabbi Burt Jacobson at the Synagogue Without Walls in Oakland, California, has created a Bar and Bat Mitzvah apprenticeship program called "Crossing the River." Rabbi Jacobson meets with small groups of students who are soon to come of age. They consider all the kinds of growing up that are happening to them. They discuss challenges in all areas of their lives, including the challenges Judaism will present for them as adults.

A thoughtful text and workbook written by Rabbi Jacobson are used. Students are encouraged, not required, to talk openly about these important subjects.

Some families consider the Bar Mitzvah a wonderful opportunity to go to Israel and decide to celebrate the ceremony there, usually at the Western Wall in Jerusalem. While many families wouldn't want to leave the circle of their relatives and community for this important event, some have found a Bar Mitzvah in Israel makes them aware of their oneness with the people Israel in all places and in all generations. The American Jewish Congress runs tours to Israel which can include Bar Mitzvah celebrations. A

*This Bar/Bat Mitzvah program was originally written by Carol Ingall of the Providence Bureau of Jewish Education and is now published by the Melton Research Center of the Jewish Theological Seminary.

travel agent can also help you make arrangements for such a trip, including the Bar Mitzvah celebration itself.

Now that you are knowledgeable about some of the Bar Mitzvah practices today, perhaps you would like to discuss them with your son or daughter. Of course, you can get all the specifics—and discuss special issues at your temple—when you talk with the rabbi or educational director.

Chapter five

Where do we belong? To join a temple (or not)

IN THE CITY where I grew up there was only one place to become Bar Mitzvah. With more than seventy thousand Jews and thirty different synagogues and temples you might think that there would have been quite a choice. But there was really only Shaarey Zedek.

Where else would the rabbi know—and mention at the service—that my great-great-uncle had been president sixty years ago, that my grandmother had belonged since marriage, and that my mother was president of the Sisterhood?

Where else was there such a large, imposing building with so many grand, wide steps in front? This was an IMPORTANT synagogue, a venerable synagogue, almost a hundred years old—a mighty age for a midwestern synagogue. Hundreds of families were proud to "be Shaarey Zedek" (as in "they're not Shaarey

Zedek"). Those wide steps were full of people after (and often during) the High Holiday services.

Yet they all seemed to know each other, and best of all they all seemed to know me. Hadn't I won the Best Queen Esther Contest there wearing an old purple evening gown given me by one of the very judges of the contest? There may have been many hundreds of members, but when my parents were late picking me up from Sunday school (and they always were) I could have gotten a ride home with anybody standing around chatting in the halls. They all seemed to have known me before I was born.

In my child's mind, so ready to see the world in black and white, it was not just that Shaarey Zedek was the utterly right synagogue. It also became apparent that all the others were so thoroughly wrong. Reform synagogues were just pretenders. They didn't even call themselves synagogues (let alone "shuls"). Instead they claimed to be temples. On top of that, they used very little Hebrew and had services at night (when it wasn't even Kol Nidre). All those Jewish men with no yarmulkas! Who did they think they were? Protestants?

But to go to a "little Orthodox shul" (who knew there could be large ones?) was probably worse. First of all, men at these shuls wore hats—not sensible, civilized yarmulkas like my father and brothers—but actual hats with brims. (Judaism was very cerebral to my family.) The men sat separate from the women because of arcane Jewish laws my mother wouldn't dream of even speaking about. In their prayerbooks they had Hebrew on both the facing pages, the sermons were often in Yiddish, and few of the members were native Detroiters.

Of course, the other Conservative synagogues were also significantly imperfect, though they had the good sense to use the same Hebrew and English prayerbook Shaarey Zedek did. The nearby one was much too young an institution, and it was full of people who still insisted on walking on Shabbat. (Our perfect synagogue had made the compromise of having insufficient parking available.)

Another Conservative synagogue nearby lacked "decorum," still another was too close to Orthodox (the women sat upstairs), and another congregation was mostly Rumanian Jews. So there was clearly only one place to belong and where your sons could be properly Bar Mitzvah. (There was hardly talk of Bat Mitzvah in 1955 in my proper and perfect synagogue.)

You may have already found the perfect and only Jewish institution (or anti-institution) for your family. You may have a place or a setting or a group where you feel comfortable with the ritual and approve of the rabbi, where you have some friends, and where your child can study, become Bar or Bat Mitzvah, and maybe even get married, God willing.

It is also possible that, even though your child is past the third grade, when kids usually begin Hebrew school, you have not yet selected a place to belong. Yet you realize you'd like, in your own way, to identify as a Jewish family. And you would like your child to come of age as a Jew. Whatever you do, don't decide it's too late or that you'd better just join a nearby temple you don't know much about. Use this opportunity to make Judaism into something meaningful and good for your family. Belonging should mean more than paying dues.

Think hard about what you've liked and disliked in your Jewish experience. You may have loved your childhood rabbi because he could really talk to kids. Perhaps you liked the sweets they had after the services. Maybe the services were so long they made you restless. Perhaps your congregation had a wonderful Purim carnival or perfect candy apples at Simchat Torah. Maybe you were mad they didn't teach you enough at religious school. (This was more common in the 1950s but is rare today.) Or you may have gone to a Jewish camp where Shabbat was really special: everyone wore white and danced and the meal was good, for a change. Perhaps you spent Seder with a family who made it fun and meaningful. Give the good and bad experiences your real, conscious attention; they'll be hiding there in the background anyway. Use them to help construct an ideal to shoot for in a congregation or Jewish group. You won't get everything you want, but at least you'll be able to look for specific things.

Temples of the same branch of Judaism will vary significantly in their traditions. Some Conservative congregations use the same prayerbook as some Orthodox congregations. Some Reform congregations are accustomed to quite traditional rituals you may not remember from a Reform childhood. It makes sense to know what you're getting into. So it is perfectly all right, in fact, downright wise, to go to services at several possible places before you decide where you'd like to belong. Visiting classes at the religious school is a good idea, too. In addition, lots of temples have open houses, another good opportunity to find out what membership might be like. (They usually advertise open houses in the local Jewish newspaper or other local papers.)

You may have very strong reasons for not joining a temple. You may live in an area with just a few Jewish families. You may want to form your own group without having to follow a path you haven't helped to make. For these and other reasons, smaller groups of Jewish families have been forming their own small congregations.

This kind of informal Jewish group has coalesced in the very Yankee town where Carol and Phil live. Four Jewish families began by celebrating some holidays together and made sure that at least every month or so they would celebrate the Shabbat together.

As children grew, they looked for a teacher who taught all the kids together at first. When more families joined in, there were enough kids for a few teachers. As of this writing, they've hired a part-time rabbi to run their new High Holiday services and to act as principal of their school. The Unitarian Church rents them space and they bring in a portable ark. (What could be more authentic?)

I always thought there would be a building fund in their future, but this group, like many others springing up all over this country, has learned to do without a synagogue. The chapel of a nearby private school is used for all their Bar and Bat Mitzvah Shabbat services, since it is large enough for all their guests. There is also an attractive, large room at the school for a party.

Often a group like this calls itself a chavurah, the Hebrew word for "company of friends." One such group in the Boston area is named the "traveling minyan." Composed of Jews who were unable to find just what they wanted in their communities, these friends banded together to find what they considered more authentic meaning springing from their own needs.

If you are part of such a group, you will probably together evolve your own way of celebrating Bar and Bat Mitzvahs for your children. And for you, this experience can be the most authentic Jewish coming of age. If the group is small enough, sometimes a chavurah will use members' homes for all their services.

Do remember that in any independent Jewish group you will be responsible for developing the Jewish identity of the group by your own exploration of ritual, law, and belief. It is a big responsibility, but it can be very satisfying and make a warm, close community, as Carol and Phil have found.

Even within a larger temple, members often want a smaller group with whom they can celebrate holidays at home. This is particularly true for individuals or nuclear families who have no other relatives nearby to share their Seder or join with for a Chanukah party. Consequently, there are now choices of chavurot (singular: chavurah) to join—or to form—at many established synagogues. Such a group of four or five families may decide to share certain holidays and possibly to study a Jewish text together.

Whatever you do, you should investigate temples or chavurot as far in advance as possible so that your child fits easily into the school and is prepared without a time crunch at the end. He'll also have more friends and history in this setting, as will you, by the time of his Bar Mitzvah.

However, if you move or realize that you have joined the wrong temple, try to change, especially before Bar Mitzvah. This is one of those decisions that must be made with integrity. A forty-year-old friend of ours is still bitter that his parents sent him to a temple they disapproved of (shorter car pool) and then dropped out the month after his Bar Mitzvah. You will find that many temples will go out of their way to help your child fit in and become educated, even if you make a somewhat late decision.

Once you've found the temple (or chavurah) you like, keep on going to services there (with or without your children; they'll get the message from your behavior). Then by the time of the Bar Mitzvah, it will really be your temple, the only and perfect place for your child to come of age as a Jew.

Chapter six

Special needs for special Bar Mitzvahs: "Raise up your child according to his needs." (Proverbs 22:6)

WE SOMETIMES WISH our children could be a little more like Benjamin Spock's model, but we regularly produce individuals. Some have differences that are relatively easy to live with, like red hair or unusual height or no sense of rhythm or a remarkable devotion to swimming.

But sometimes they have differences that make life more complicated or even difficult and painful. There are lovely Jewish children who are visually or hearing impaired. There are nice Jewish kids who stutter or who speak with difficulty or who find reading very hard. There are beloved Jewish children with Down's syndrome, and there are those who must use crutches because of cerebral palsy or orthopedic problems.

All these children, like all Jewish children of twelve and thirteen everywhere, will be or have been Bar Mitzvah. As I already pointed out, you become Bar Mitzvah at thirteen if you're a boy, and Bat Mitzvah at twelve if you're a girl, simply by becoming that age if you're Jewish. The specific traditions have developed over the centuries, but they are only traditions, not law. They have the same force as the traditions for naming a baby. The Ashkenazic Jews customarily name their children after a relative who has died. The Sephardim name theirs for a living relative. Many parents consult rabbis about what they are "allowed" to name children, but there is no law, just tradition. And the same is true for Bar and Bat Mitzvahs.

So, if you have a child with special needs, you can work to shape the service and celebration of his Bar Mitzvah in a way that is appropriate for your family. Whatever you do, be assured that it will be quite lawful according to Judaism, as long as your child has reached the appropriate age.

The Bar or Bat Mitzvah education and ceremony will be uniquely important for a child with special needs. More than most other kids, these youngsters rarely get a chance to shine, to be the star, the best, the prettiest, to have the best grade or the best part. The Bar or Bat Mitzvah is a perfect and unique opportunity for a child to be appreciated for what he CAN do, instead of being shut out for what he can't. He or she will also get the opportunity to have the glamor, attention, and fun that come with being center stage. Beautiful clothes are selected, hairdresser appointments kept, relatives arrive from faraway places, menus are planned—all in honor of this beloved child.

While the experience is wonderful because it is unique, it is also grand because it is regular. By celebrating his Bar Mitzvah he shares an important experience open to all his Jewish peers and his siblings. He or she has the opportunity to participate fully in the most important rite of passage for a Jewish child just as all Jewish children do. Teachers and parents find that children with special needs treat this important occasion with great seriousness and savor the formal opportunity to become an adult and to

friends, teachers, neighbors; and this event showed us all that Andrea could lead a satisfying life." I hope the temple that didn't think it could serve Andrea realizes what a wonderful family it lost.

All this sensible progress in Jewish education doesn't mean you won't run into a rabbi who will give you a hard time. It gets you right in the heart when someone would deny your child something valuable. But you know that this kind of rabbi is just not educated about Jewish tradition. Try to educate him. It will surely make you mad if you have to, but don't give up.

And, if one person at a temple says no, ask another. (It is not really a temple if it doesn't have factions.) If one temple can't accommodate you, find another. Or see if you can hire a teacher or rabbinic student to educate your child and plan and run your service. After all, the fundamental meaning of rabbi is teacher, and that is all you need.

Chapter seven

The Bar Mitzvah book: What did I do with the cleaning slip with the bandleader's name on the back?

YOU USED TO be pleased to find a large, hand-addressed envelope in your mail box. *A party!* you would smile to yourself. Now, however, you find yourself casting a cold, critical eye at the lettering and the colors this hostess chose; the Bar Mitzvah research has begun.

The last time you were involved with a large social event, probably all you had to do was stand still while they hemmed your veil. Your mother made all the lists. Now it's your turn.

By this time in your life, lists are second nature to you. There are probably five or six in your purse right now and at least one in the pocket of your sweatsuit. So you are going to be right in your element planning this Bar Mitzvah, which is, in some ways, just list-making on a grand scale. But do find a home for all your Bar Mitzvah-related lists.

Get yourself a blank notebook, preferably one with pockets. Now you've got some place to jot down all your ideas, lists, and research. You won't need to try to remember everything. You won't have to hunt through your pockets for little slips of paper. Put the little slips of paper in the pockets of your notebook.

I suggest the following categories for your notebook divisions:

guest list
service (aliyot, prayers to learn, requirements of dress)
caterer
menu
accommodations and maps for out-of-towners
invitations
sundries
    cleaning help
    candy
    flowers
    music
    paper goods

Now, put your name and address on the book. Then when you leave it at the florist's and he finds it in the violets, he'll know it's yours. You might also want to think of a place at home where you'll usually leave it.

Do write down any phone number you think you'll need, even if you know you'll be calling only once. This is because there is no such thing as calling once. The stationery store's telephone will be busy, the florist's tape recording machine will garble your message, and the candy lady will be too busy taking chocolates out of the oven even to write down your number. Write them all down in the book; you're bound to call again.

Just by putting all the information in one place, you'll find that some decisions get made by themselves. Seeing it all in black and white makes you begin to face facts like numbers and prices and logistical possibilities.

Speaking of numbers, it's time to start on the guest list.

Chapter eight

The guest list: But there are 125 just in Michael's family!

THERE COMES A TIME when every person you run into in the grocery store is cause for reappraisal. *Will we invite them to the Bar Mitzvah?* you wonder as you sort through the tomatoes. Or sometimes, *Will we have to invite them?*

There follow brief discussions with your husband, who says such helpful things as "Who are they?" and "Let's just invite her. I can't stand him."

You are beginning to cast that same critical eye at your car pools, your colleagues, and even your relatives. You better start writing their names down.

Just write them all down—the definites, the maybe's, the do-we-have-to's, all the levels of relatives, and the they-invited-us-es. To make sure you don't forget someone, take a careful look through your personal telephone directory.

53

After a while, with all these lists piling up, you'll want to count up. You are very likely to find that you have between seventy-five and one hundred and fifty on your list. Whatever the number, just putting together the list and doing the addition will help you move forward in your planning.

You may find that you don't like the size of the party you've come up with. This will cause you to evolve criteria for your guest list. I suggest the following:

1. People who will be happy to share the occasion.
2. Family. Some will be happy, some won't. But they all contribute to your child's history and identity.
3. Age appropriateness. Small children are very often bored and irritable at an adult religious and social occasion. There may well be certain small children you wouldn't dream of leaving out, but there are others who will only make guests (especially their parents) miserable. As Emily Post suggests when children are excluded from a wedding, you might enclose a note with the parents' invitation explaining that you couldn't include all the children you might have liked to. It is also nice, if you can, to include such children in another related festivity, like a brunch for the family the Sunday morning after the Bar Mitzvah.
4. Obligations:
   a. They invited you and you should invite them even though you know this will set up an unending series of obligations. If these people are bound to be a part of your life, don't fight it, invite them. Keep this group small.
   b. You or your husband works/carpools/jogs with them, and you know it will be awkward before, during, and after the Bar Mitzvah if you haven't invited them. Besides, then you won't have to keep avoiding the subject.
5. Teachers, both religious and secular, who have been important to you and your child. If a young person is going to declare himself an adult, it seems only fitting that those who helped form him should be present. Similarly, the rabbi and cantor, who probably had a good deal to do with your child's

religious education, ought to be invited. It is a matter of local custom and their busy weekend schedules whether they will come to the party. Most come for at least a glass of wine and a mazel tov, but all ought to be honored with the invitation.

6. Those who are of historical importance to your child, like a former favorite babysitter and the rabbi who married you and your husband.

7. Friends of the family. Even a four-year-old deserves to have his best friend present for such a big day. It will make life easier for you. You might also include a sitter for younger children, or you can deputize an uncle or cousin.

8. Friends of the Bar Mitzvah boy. The Bar Mitzvah boy will have firm ideas about which friends and acquaintances to invite. Some surprise their parents by writing a very short list. One I know invited just boys. Remember, Bar and Bat Mitzvahs haven't lived long enough to have that many friends. Moreover, an invitation sent to a member of the opposite sex may have an awesome significance that a seventh grader can't handle. Finally, do keep in mind that the whole thing happens at an age which many of us would like to forget.

I urge you to follow your youngster's lead, but be ready for alterations. You'll be able to smooth things out for him and teach him some useful social lessons along the way. For instance, it is perfectly okay to call the mother of a sweet young thing who suddenly the week before the Bar Mitzvah must be added to the list. You *can* call and act like you sent an invitation and you're surprised she hasn't responded. Or you can simply tell the truth in a reasonably diplomatic way: "David realized that he left Lisa's name off the list and he's sorry and hoping she can come, even at this late date." The same can be done, of course, for adults whom you regret forgetting to invite.

After all the criteria are considered, my strong advice is to err on the side of inviting too many guests. This will, in the end, make you happy and it isn't nearly as extravagant as it sounds.

First, one must crassly keep in mind that not everyone who is invited is going to come. Perfectly nice friends turn out to have a chance to spend only that one week in California, at company expense, and very sadly have to miss your son's Bar Mitzvah. Some dear old pal you went to kindergarten with writes an enthusiastic acceptance note and sends a wonderful present well in advance. Then she lands in the hospital the day before.

But there is an even more important reason for inviting the maybe's. You're likely to be really sorry on the Bar Mitzvah day if you don't. There were two potential guests I decided I shouldn't invite because I just wasn't close enough to them. I even pondered inviting them the day before. And I should have.

Chapter nine

The place of your reception: A tent is not so good in November.

ONE OF MY FAVORITE parts of the Shabbat services is the announcements near the end. You get to find out which rabbi has his mother-in-law visiting, when the haggadot go on sale at the Sisterhood gift shop, whether there's something appealing at the adult education, and which senator we'd better write to about the Soviet Jews. And then you are told where "the Bar Mitzvah family will greet their guests" . . . which is to say, where the party will be.

There are, at my temple, only three choices. The temple president announces that the family will greet their guests

1. in the community hall,
2. at their home, or
3. at the place of their reception.

"The place of their reception" is code for the fact that the party will be held at a restaurant, club, hotel or other secular location.

Such a place is not identified by name. It is axiomatic at our temple that a Jewish religious event ought to be celebrated at a Jewish place. An obvious corollary to this is that the place should be kosher. So, even if you are having your celebration at the snazziest restaurant in town, it does not deserve advertisement at the service. You should have a lovely time, but better if it had been at the temple.

The values implicit in this announcement have always endeared the temple to me. A Jewish occasion belongs in a Jewish place. There's nothing more Jewish than a Jewish home; but if yours can't accommodate as many guests as you want, the temple is the right place for the festivity.

Most temples are built with celebrations as well as services in mind. Not every one has a bride's room, but most do have a large hall intended for parties. They have the tables, the dishes, the kitchen equipment, electrical wattage, and usually a great deal of experience with excited party-givers. You can provide your own good associations with the building in which, by Bar Mitzvah time, you are likely to feel quite at home.

Here you can also confer quite easily with the rabbi, his secretary, the executive director, and the custodian—not so for the maitre d' at the Hotel Plaza Astoria or even the captain of the busboys.

The temple is exactly the right place to celebrate your child's Bar Mitzvah. Here is where he studied and where he fooled around with his friends, got delivered by his many car pools, and attended services; and here he will recite the Torah blessings for the first time as a man, in the company of the congregation. His father may have gone to Yale, but the flavor of the Yale Club, while top drawer and quite elegant, is unlikely to be appropriate.

You will also discover some humane facts about your temple; it may turn out to have a ramp to the side door so Great-Aunt Louise can attend without the fuss and embarrassment of being carried. Most likely you can drop by almost anytime to check out the colors of the curtains to make sure you aren't ordering flowers or napkins that clash.

It is also fair to point out that temples can raise some problems for Bar Mitzvah parents. You may want to save money by making some of the food yourself; however, your temple's kashrut requirements may prevent you from serving food you've made at home. This is rarely true at Reform temples, and some Conservative synagogues will allow you to prepare food in their kitchens even if you can't bring food from home.

In a temple which observes kashrut, you will also be limited to the list of caterers approved by the temple. There will also be a small fee for the mashgiach (ritual supervisor).

You should certainly consider having your Bar Mitzvah celebration at home, if you think you have enough space for your guests. In an eight-room home like mine, it is appropriate to plan on no more than about forty guests. Apprehensively, I planned on one hundred and fifteen guests; my fear was confirmed by the dispassionate professional judgment of a very experienced cateress. She took a hard look around and assured me that my guests would be quite miserable and would stay only a short time. Of course, you may have a larger home.

Let me add that I have been to a wonderful, intimate, catered buffet Bat Mitzvah luncheon for forty in a normal-sized house. The family was small and wanted to have just close friends. We all stayed all afternoon, and we all talked in an easy, friendly way that is possible only at small parties. Stephanie, the young woman of the hour, showed us her presents, took off her shoes, and was very much part of the party. There is much to be said for such a celebration.

If you want to expand the party space at home, someone will undoubtedly suggest a tent. You can rent a very large canvas tent with a wooden floor. The tent can enclose much of your yard. Tents are, however, expensive: four hundred dollars and more, and extra for the floor.

If you turn out to have absolutely perfect weather (72 degrees all afternoon), tents are pleasant and they do add privacy and you can dance on the floor. They can shield you from the sun and, with the sides up, they allow a breeze. However, when the weather is hot and muggy, I have always found them stuffy. If the weather is cold or rainy, they offer insufficient protection, and your guests are likely to be uncomfortable. This is true even though the tent-renters can provide heaters; the heat will be uneven and it won't feel comfortably warm anywhere. You also have the anticipatory anxiety of worrying about the weather. While you can call the florist or the caterer to change something or to consult, the weather bureau is just a recording.

Which brings me to air conditioning. If your celebration will occur in any month which might possibly be hot, take that possibility seriously. Don't let a wet blanket of heat and humidity fall on your beautiful day.

Though I am obviously very strongly in favor of a home or synagogue celebration for a Jewish occasion, there are times when this is just not possible. Ann and David celebrated the brit of their son on an Indian reservation where David was stationed for the Public Health Service. It was a wonderful, joyous party, complete with lox and mohel brought in from Phoenix. Many relatives flew all the way across the country to be there, but no one enjoyed it more than the Navajos, who take rites of passage even more seriously than Jews do.

Similarly, there are authentic Jewish celebrations of Bar Mitzvahs which happen outside temples. Cindy and Fred, who loved their summers at camp, especially because they met there, always sent their kids to that same Jewish camp. Ever since their son was born on July 14 many years ago, they knew they'd celebrate his Bar Mitzvah at camp.

The camp is, by the way, not a Hebrew-speaking camp, just a Jewish camp where the kids learn how to rotate in volleyball, do the jay stroke in canoeing, and compete madly for the blue and the gold during color war. But, on Friday night the camp has Shabbat dinner and on Saturday morning it holds Shabbat services.

So, last July, bearing a delicious combination of catered and homemade food, the family and friends arrived to celebrate a beautiful rustic Bar Mitzvah at the lodge. The camaraderie and youth of the campers and staff made it an especially festive celebration. It was one time every kid wished that he, too, had a summer birthday.

Finally, it can just turn out that you have to have the Bar Mitzvah celebration in a secular place. Your temple may have no social hall. If your temple schedules two Bar Mitzvahs on the same date and has only one social hall, you might not get there first or you might lose the toss.

It is, therefore, wise to request the use of the social hall well in advance, but always be flexible. We reserved the hall and got the caterer signed up, the Torah and haftarah portions were half-learned, and a major snag developed. Someone remembered that one thousand chairs would be bolted to the floor of the social hall on our Saturday in anticipation of Rosh Hashanah services a few days later. We did get another day and the social hall but not without a week of mild hysteria.

Some people just find the social hall totally unesthetic. Some want to celebrate in ways that are unacceptable to the temple. Perhaps you want ballroom dancing and the temple doesn't allow it on Shabbat. Or you want candlelighting but the temple prohibits lighting fires of Shabbat. I fully support these two restrictions, which my temple enforces. But what kind of temple is it if there aren't some members vehemently opposed to one or another of its rules? . . . Two Jews, three opinions.

You should be aware of certain problems that can arise from using a secular location, which is often a public and commercial place. First, you'll need to work harder to make the celebration consistent with the ceremony if you are celebrating at a public place. Your Bar or Bat Mitzvah child will easily detect the disparity between a religious service in the morning and a purely social occasion in the afternoon. Nobody is as sensitive to hypocrisy as a teenager. Second, a hotel or restaurant reception may exclude observant guests because of their kashrut observance or because they would have to ride from the temple to the celebration.

In addition, strangers, through accident, curiosity, or even malice, may inject themselves into your party. At best, this can interfere with an easy intimacy among guests. At worst, it can be very unsettling. A year or so ago we attended a Bar Mitzvah celebration at a nice local restaurant. While the guests were clapping to the music of a horah danced by a circle of the kids, a stranger in an unfamiliar army uniform materialized and began clapping loudly and shouting. The host and maitre d' removed him at once but not before the guests became quite uncomfortable.

Another problem can be the complexity of transportation arrangements between temple and party. Jerry's party was twenty minutes away from the temple, which didn't seem too bad. However, this twenty minutes of driving was preceded by at least a half an hour of pairing carless out-of-towners with local guests—all this while everyone was busy educating each other ad nauseam about the best way to get to the hotel. Much of the good feeling generated in the service had disappeared by the time we all reconvened.

Your Bar or Bat Mitzvah may very much want to have his or her very own party, just for kids, in addition to the family's celebration. Soft drinks, chips, and a DJ may be your child's idea of having made it across the passage to adulthood. The disc jockey could be an older teen who plays the tapes and works some cool (as opposed to motherly) wonders at getting the kids to dance.

Though it isn't particularly Jewish to sip soft drinks and dance to incomprehensible lyrics and very loud music, there is something very right about honoring your child's wish for a celebration for just his friends. Many kids wouldn't dream of having such a party, and I would never initiate it. But I'd certainly let someone who is declaring his adulthood have the pleasure of serving as host at his own kind of party, if he wants it. Invite a couple of your friends to keep you company in the background so you can enjoy this event with an appropriate detachment.

My husband converted to Judaism as an adult; he became Bar Mitzvah at age thirty-one at a regular Shabbat morning service. We celebrated at a luncheon in a friend's apartment—just five of us who were close friends. There was wonderful food, good conversation, and a lot of laughs; everyone was honored to be part of the occasion. Van was the first person any of us knew who had chosen to be Bar Mitzvah as an adult, and we all felt very moved— and almost historic. It wouldn't have been appropriate to have the hoopla you get at thirteen, but he did get a lot of fountain pens.

Chapter ten

The festive meal is served: You mean it's $18.90 per person, not including the waitresses and tablecloths?

WHEN WE WERE in the throes of selecting a festive meal, my old friend Karen suggested solving the whole problem by just sending out an announcement that said:

> Mr. and Mrs. Van Lanckton
> are pleased to announce
> that they can afford
> two hot hors d'oeuvres
> and the standard buffet
> without the Viennese sweet table.

Though this would appear to be a crass solution, there are days, as the estimates mount, when you think you'll just forget the whole thing. Or, the thought crosses your mind, maybe you'll copy the fanciest debutante parties and have sixteen watercress sandwiches.

What kind of craziness is this, you think, *a three-hour party for a small fortune?* Surely Judaism didn't intend to inflict poverty on Bar Mitzvah parents.

Actually the festive Bar Mitzvah meal has been a traditional part of the occasion for hundreds of years. A seudat mitzvah, or festive meal, celebrating a commandment is customary for several occasions. You are probably most familiar with the seudah at a wedding, brit, or Bar Mitzvah. However, it is also traditional to have such a festivity at the completion of the study of some religious book. Religious schools these days have revived this tradition and often celebrate with food and song when a class finishes a book or receives their first prayerbook.

However customary it is to celebrate these important passages, it is also venerable tradition to celebrate in an appropriate manner. Medieval rabbis forbade Bar Mitzvah festivities that were ostentatious and extravagant. In seventeenth-century Poland they even decreed how much jewelry you could wear to a social function. And, at the same time in Lithuania, the rabbis wrote:

> Inasmuch as people are spending too much money unnecessarily on festive meals, every Jewish community and settlement that has a rabbi is expected to assemble its officers and rabbi to consider the number of guests which it is suitable for every individual, in view of his wealth and the occasion, to invite to a festive meal. . . .*

Rabbis required such restraint because of their own disapproval and also because of their fear of anti-Jewish criticism for such ostentation. We all remember (with horror, I hope) when *Time* magazine reported on a Bar Mitzvah staged at the Orange Bowl.

My husband conveyed a modern version of the sumptuary laws

---

*Sharon and Michael Strassfeld, eds., *The Second Jewish Catalog* (Philadelphia: Jewish Publication Society, 1976), p. 65.

when he responded to my concern over whether two hot hors d'oeuvres would be enough. "You might as well take it easy," he said, "we aren't going to win the napkin-folding contest anyway." Which is to say, no matter what you serve, how you decorate, what entertainment you provide, someone will have had it already or done something more unusual. The only sensible thing to do is to try to figure out how to celebrate in a way that is authentic for you and your family.

Authenticity will reflect your family's own values, style and traditions, the size of your guest list, and the size of your budget. It may mean standing up against some of the local conventions, but you are more likely to end up feeling at home at your own child's celebration and not overly depressed at the thought of the impending bills.

But, you may say, you have absolutely no idea how much any possible celebration costs. Asking people how much they paid for something ranks even lower than asking them how much they weigh. So you are probably most reluctant to ask friends, unless they are very dear ones, what their Bar Mitzvah celebration cost. Only one couple, very old friends, ever got up the courage to ask us, and that was just as they were about to leave for home, two hundred miles away. But if there is someone you can ask, do.

In case you can't, here are some examples of the range of prices in the Boston area in 1985. Do remember, though, the prices change every time it rains in sunny California.

A popular kosher caterer who cooks at your temple charges about $20 to $25 per person for a sumptuous, varied dairy buffet. This includes everything except liquor or wine and whatever the temple charges for the room and dishes. Following is the specific menu Jackie and Glenda of J & G Caterers, Brockton, Massachusetts, prepared for the party following our son's Bar Mitzvah:

hot hors d'oeuvres
   little pizzas
   potato pancakes
   stuffed mushrooms

cold hors d'oeuvres
  gefilte fishballs
  herring salad
  herring tidbits
challah
sponge cake, honey cake
buffet
  egg, tuna, fish salad on lettuce leaves
  stuffed tomatoes
  spinach pie
  quiche
  noodle pudding
  assorted cheeses
  assorted bagels and rolls
  cream cheese and lox
  strawberries and sour cream
  tossed salad
dessert
  assorted mini-Danish
  pick-up pastries (torts, eclairs, and rumballs)

Kosher deli trays, full of all kinds of delicious meats, breads, salads, and condiments, cost $5 a person. You'll need more than one tray since the largest serves twenty-five guests. You must also pay for room rental, dishes, serving persons, and drinks.

At the other extreme, a fancy downtown hotel (not kosher but where you can get a dairy meal acceptable to some traditional Jews) charges from $28 to $37 per person for a served luncheon. In addition, there is a 17 percent service charge and, in Massachusetts, a 5 percent meals tax, for a total with service charge and tax of about $34 to $45 per person. Moreover, you must pay (a lot) to rent the room and more for the dance floor, hors d'oeuvres, and liquor.

This is a very good time to have a relative in the business. Whether you do or you don't, it makes sense first to consider carefully what you would like if you could have whatever you wanted. Perhaps you've always liked the idea of a light lunch with champagne. This can be very charming and elegant and not nearly as expensive as a sit-down roast beef meal. On the other hand, you may feel it is awfully rude not to give someone a large meal if he has come all the way from Albuquerque to celebrate your child's Bar Mitzvah.

Do you want to be unlimited in the number of guests and offer simpler refreshments, perhaps just a kiddush? Are you more comfortable with informality? Would you like to have a served luncheon because it extends the party over the whole afternoon and evening? Do you like a varied buffet because then there's always something for everyone?

It is obvious that you'll reduce the cost of the food by preparing some of it yourself. Friends may wish to help as well, and that is a lovely token of friendship, if you ask me. As I mentioned, each temple has its own rules for the use of the kitchen. But if you can use the temple kitchen, you'll be able to take advantage of a setting prepared for quantity cooking. There are cookbooks intended just for such occasions.

A tried and true choice is a well-known Jewish caterer. How do you find such a creature if your entertaining has ranged from an occasional dinner for eight to one cake baked from a mix and served after miniature golf? First you ask anyone you know who might have used a caterer. You can supplement that by asking your temple for a list. In fact, your temple is likely to send you a list if it requires only kosher food. You can augment that by checking the ads, usually on the wedding announcement page, in the Jewish weekly newspaper for your area.

Many caterers will send you sample menus and prices. Some want to make an appointment in person. Whatever happens, don't let them intimidate you. Believe me, they want your business. Since you have thought about what you would like, you are no one to be pushed around. That doesn't mean you don't have an open mind; it just means that you know enough to look askance at an overly heavy meal at an overly heavy price.

Don't hesitate to investigate caterers nobody has used before. I decided it wouldn't hurt to call a wonderful French restaurant in Boston and found that, indeed, the owner would be glad to come to my home to see about catering our son's Bar Mitzvah party. I picked her up at the trolley early one morning, and we spent a most useful and pleasant morning together. She came armed with several possible French and Eastern European menus.

Although the menus were wonderful, the prices were steep. I didn't end up hiring her, but she always comes out of the kitchen to say hello when my husband and I go to her restaurant for dinner. She makes me feel like visiting royalty. So much for intimidation. Really great people, my mother always assured me, are humble.

By the way, this very same restaurant owner once koshered her entire kitchen for a Bar Mitzvah celebration, at the expense of the family, of course. This is out of my class, but it does give you an interesting sense of the possibilities.

A word is in order for getting along with your caterer. Do take into account his personality before you decide to hire him. If he is curt with you and always irritated at your questions, he may spoil some of your fun before and at the party. So you'd better really think his crepes are worth it if it means having to put up with arrogance or rudeness. After all, he should have developed some finesse at dealing with hostesses who care about their parties.

I knew that Jackie was the right one for me because, whenever I panicked, she was calm, rational, and pleasant; she assured me that she had never lost a mother yet.

Chapter eleven

Second thoughts: The reluctant Bar Mitzvah

ALMOST EVERY Bar or Bat Mitzvah will have at least moments of ambivalence. These moments may come as early as when Hebrew school begins to compete with Little League or baton twirling. They may come later when performance anxiety grows as the child realizes he is going to have to demonstrate his education and commitment in an awfully public way. He may also begin to question God or organized religion or the trouble of being a persecuted minority—just as the guest list is being assembled.

Whatever his issues, take them very seriously. Put that guest list away for a while. Give your child plenty of time to talk with you, his dad, his rabbi, a teacher, or anyone else who can help. Let him know that these are venerable, worthwhile, and understandable concerns. Above all, try not to panic because of your investment in his Bar Mitzvah. You won't die if he doesn't become Bar Mitzvah, but something between you will die if you and he don't try to understand and work out his concerns.

As for ambivalence to Hebrew school, it is likely to be milder if you are yourself quite confident (but not always). You owe it to yourself and your child to consider very carefully the value of his religious education. A serious and thoughtful reflection on your feelings about Judaism can help you—and help you help your child.

Don't be hesitant to monitor the quality of his religious education either. Visit the classes; speak to the teacher, the principal, or the rabbi. Join the school committee. Work to make sure he's getting a good religious education. You'd certainly step right in to his public or private school if he turned against long division.

I also suggest that you be reasonably flexible about occasional absence from Hebrew school when a crucial Little League game is played. I found this all very perplexing myself when my son asked for the first time to miss Hebrew school for a game. An older and wiser colleague assured me that all her four boys had graduated from Hebrew school and played Little League as well. In fact, they all went to Hebrew high school, too.

If your child feels intense stage fright about his Bar Mitzvah, do whatever you can that he will allow to make it easier for him. Arrange for extra practice or tutoring. Help him write his speech, showing great appreciation for his efforts and understanding. Listen to him practice, concentrating on how much he has learned and how much you love him. Remind him that everyone makes mistakes and that ceremonies go right on in spite of them. This is such a self-conscious time that it will be hard for him to believe you. Still, you need to convey your confidence in him any way you can.

If your child has important religious questions, this is a wonderful time to begin discussing them together and reading more to educate yourself. This kind of education goes on, of course, most weeks at Shabbat services (and Jewish adult education classes, too). However, the questions of an adolescent might spur you to some reading of your own. (There's a book list for you in the appendix.) There's nothing wrong with asking the school to deal with some of these questions, either. Most rabbis I know would welcome an honest, challenging discussion with adolescents about God and Judaism.

In any Jewish exploration of religious questions, you might find it useful to keep in mind this wonderful line from Elie Wiesel's *Night*: "Man raises himself toward God by the questions he asks Him."* Elie Wiesel spent his adolescence in concentration camps and has become the most eloquent witness to the Holocaust. Yet he continues to write and teach, searching for truth and goodness. Perhaps knowing about Elie Wiesel and his questions will help your teenager realize that it is fine to study and become Bar Mitzvah without possessing perfect faith.

Students of mine often used to complain that they found nothing they wanted at Sunday school: they were there only because of their parents. I used to feel compelled to explain at great length why religious school was useful for the students themselves, putting to one side their parents' wishes. But the older I get, the more impressed I am with another principal I once overheard. She was dealing with a snippy young thing who was sent to the office for disrupting class. "I'm only here because my parents make me come," she whined. "I think that's a very good reason," the principal replied.

Sometimes what seems like anger at religion turns out to be something quite different. Some kids of divorced parents, for instance, become very anxious about their Bar Mitzvahs; two antagonistic groups will be coming together with only this one thirteen-year-old to unite them. If you think this might be behind your child's rejection of Bar Mitzvah, listen to these concerns and try to talk it out with him, and with your ex-spouse, if you can. The rabbi ought to be able to help, too, since this situation comes up often. A child shouldn't have to bear this kind of responsibility, even if he is coming of age. He should be reassured about that well in advance.

*Elie Weisel, *Night* (New York: Avon Books, 1969), p. 14.

It happens in even the best families that a child may simply refuse to become Bar Mitzvah. "I think that now, at sixteen, she's beginning to find her way back to Judaism," a mother recently told me of her daughter, who was unwilling three years ago to become Bat Mitzvah. The mother, an outstanding Hadassah worker, wishes now that she had let Aliza drop out of Hebrew school earlier. "It took a lot of sessions with a psychiatrist to work this out for myself," the mother told me.

Adolescence, as I hope we all remember from our own, is also a time when children need to assert themselves and stand up to their parents. Bar Mitzvah is sometimes one of the testing grounds. Try very hard to be open-minded about your child's feelings toward his Bar Mitzvah. Keep remembering yourself at thirteen. Allow flexibility where it is possible and reasonable. Where is it written that he has to lead the whole service just because his brother did? There's no law that says it must be a blue suit or the longest Torah portion or a menu that includes only foods that adults will like. Respect and appreciation for a maturing child's wishes will make this a more meaningful event for everyone involved.

Chapter twelve

Invitations: Emily Post meets the Talmud.

EVEN THOUGH she is the friendliest person I know, you may not have met my friend Miriam. And that is a shame, especially if you are going to be selecting Bar Mitzvah invitations soon. Miriam has saved all the invitations she has ever received. She stuffs them in a kitchen drawer and can pop them out at a moment's notice so you can put them in a bag, take them home, and sift through to find one you like.

Of course, you can collect your own, but Miriam does have an edge, since she teaches the Bar Mitzvah year at Hebrew school and her students usually invite her to their Bar Mitzvahs. She had high motivation to save the invitations since she has three children of her own to bring of age.

Invitations are the first tangible indication that this event is actually going to happen. They also set the tone for your celebration. And, once you order them, the die is cast. You are going to have boxes of them to address; it's going to be very important that what you selected six weeks before will not make you wince when multiplied by one hundred and twenty-five.

You will find sample invitations at stationery and party stores and at Jewish bookstores, in addition to the stationery section of department stores. You can also consult with local calligraphers who advertize in the Jewish press, in Jewish bookstores, in temple newsletters, and on temple bulletin boards. Your rabbi or religious school principal may also be able to recommend a calligrapher. (Sample invitations are in the appendix.)

It would be nicest and most personal if you could handwrite an invitation to each guest; if your list is small enough, you can do just that. You can also telephone your invitation. Most families inform their relatives and close friends of the date well in advance to avoid any conflict. However, the great majority of Bar Mitzvah parents also send printed invitations about four weeks before the date.

These days, as Americans have become more comfortable with their ethnic origins, Bar Mitzvah invitations sometimes include some Hebrew or a narrative explaining what the Bar Mitzvah ceremony is. At any rate, people no longer feel tied to the Emily Post formal wedding invitation as their model. As in all other decisions for this occasion, you'll probably end up happiest using what pleases you. That won't necessarily mean the pink foil invitations that your daughter's best friend sent.

I was happy only with the Emily Post formal kind, though they're rarely used. We did modify them by using our first names rather than Mr. and Mrs.

In 1985 in major Boston stores, all of which seem to have the same catalogs, prices for one hundred printed invitations ranged from $90 to $190. You can arrange to spend more money by having them engraved or elaborately decorated, but I wouldn't. You don't want your friends to think they're opening a perfume ad from Bloomingdale's.

As you can see, I'm not all that open-minded about what kind of invitations to order. And I am entirely close-minded about response cards. Any person who needs a check-off card and self-addressed stamped envelope in order to remember to tell me that he will come to my son's Bar Mitzvah shouldn't have been invited. A guest of mine should enjoy the call or note to me to tell me how much he's looking forward to this occasion.

Indented at the right, below the main message on the invitation, should be the words "Please reply" or "R.S.V.P." Any invitee worth his two hot hors d'oeuvres should know how to handle that. In addition to being the appropriate way to request a response, this method will save you many dollars you don't need to spend.

By the way, when you or your children receive invitations to Bar Mitzvahs, keep in mind how it feels to be the one sending them. Respond immediately and with enthusiasm, and teach your children to do the same. In an age when both parents are often out working, it is a good idea to send a note rather than to call. It may be hard to reach your hostess by phone, and a child may take the message imperfectly or forget to relay it. If you send a prompt note, your hostess can plan much more easily and she knows you're eager to come.

Back to the invitations. If you employ a calligrapher, he will use a process of reproduction called photo offset. If you use a printer, he'll give you a choice between printing, raised printing, and engraving. I would definitely choose the raised printing since it looks much better than the printing, in fact, darn near as nice as engraving. The price for raised printing is much more reasonable than that for engraving.

It is no longer necessary or stylish to use an outer envelope as well as an inner envelope, even for wedding invitations. It wastes both trees and money. If you are determined to add to the cost of the envelopes, you may have a return address imprinted on the back flap of each. Of course, you can simply write it on yourself when you address the invitations.

A good compromise is to have made and use an embosser. This clever gadget imprints (without ink) your return address in raised letters on the envelope flap. You can order one for under twenty-five dollars at any fine stationery store; it will certainly speed up the invitations and all your other correspondence.

While the printer is busy with the invitations, now is the time for you to assemble your address box. I know you already have a Bar Mitzvah book (see chapter seven) and you've put some addresses in there and you know how to find the rest of them easily. Anyway, why did I tell you to make a book if it's really a box you need?

The address box, you see, is not just for you. It is also for your child, who will soon be King or Queen of the Thank-You Notes. This box is going to include everything anyone needs to know to address the invitations, record the responses, and get the thank-you notes written. This is because each guest (or pair of guests or family of guests) will have an index card which will list:

> guest's name (last name first)
> name Bar Mitzvah person should use in thank-you note (in
>   parentheses)
> guest's name, as it should appear on envelope (Mr., Mrs., Dr.,
>   Ms.)
> guest's address
> space at bottom for gift received

The card will look like this when it is completed:

> Diamond, Elizabeth (Aunt Liz)
> Ms. Elizabeth Diamond
> 112 Oak Street
> Buffalo, NY 18455
> fountain pen

These cards should be filed alphabetically using dividers for each letter. Get a second set of alphabet dividers and put them behind all those nicely alphabetized cards. Then, as each guest responds, you can (1) put a check in the corner of the card to indicate that the guest has responded and (2) put those who have accepted into the second alphabet, which will become your actual guest list.

As each gift arrives, you or your child can enter it on the appropriate card and check off the gift when the note has been written. It is unlikely that you'll receive many gifts before the Bar Mitzvah and extremely unlikely that your child will have the time before the event to thank the givers. So you keep the box till the Bar Mitzvah celebration is over, and then you hand it and the responsibility for thank-you notes to your child, now adult. (Pointers on helping your son or daughter get the notes written promptly and properly appear in chapter eighteen.)

The Post Office insists that zip codes are crucial in getting the mail delivered. You may need to consult with said Post Office in order to get zip codes for some of your guests' addresses. Every zip code in the United States is listed in an immense book in your Post Office on the counter with the dry pens. Bring your own pen and the list of addresses you need to complete.

Speaking of pens, this is a nice time to buy yourself a decent one. I know that everyone thinks a Bar Mitzvah boy needs a pen or two, but his mother needs one first. I even went so far as to buy myself a fountain pen, since I thought it would improve my writing on the invitations. At least, make sure you have something better than a ballpoint pen that leaves behind blobs of ink.

Chapter thirteen

Music, etc.: One man's Haifa Swinging Singers is another man's Grateful Dead.

THE MUSIC AT Henry's Bar Mitzvah party was excruciatingly loud, full of screaming rock lyrics, and the whole room vibrated from the noise.

Since Henry's mother and I have been friends for many years, it was a real treat to be with her and her family for the Bar Mitzvah. I've known Henry since he was a baby, and so it was especially dramatic to see him celebrate his Bar Mitzvah; with his beautiful voice, the haftarah was wonderful. At the party, the food was delicious, interesting but not too rich and fancy, just the way I like it. And we were seated at a very nice table of old friends. It was just that it was hard to talk over that music.

When I saw Henry's dad, Steve, at a Little League game the next week, I told him how much I enjoyed the day. I enumerated the wonderful elements, carefully leaving out the band. Steve chimed

THE BAR MITZVAH MOTHER'S MANUAL

right in, saying, "Like I always say, it's a great band and great people that make a party great."

There must be no disputing over tastes. For a Bar Mitzvah celebration, you and Steve and I all deserve to have our kind of music. This can be a little complicated even within a family, since children don't always like the same music their parents like. However, unless you are seriously into madrigals and your child is devoted only to acid rock, you will probably be able to find some musical fare that will reasonably suit you both. This is likely because musicians who play for parties are used to playing a broad range.

You can acquaint yourself with what is available in your area by consulting the cantor, musical director, choral director, or music teacher at your temple or at your child's school. Since musicians tend to know each other, all of the above are likely to know what is available in both secular and Jewish music.

Then talk to the musicians. This is harder than it sounds. Musicians are on a different schedule than the rest of the world. They are also artists and so not heavily involved in prosaic things like returning calls. But they do usually have tapes to answer their phones, and quite interesting tapes at that, with Haydn in the background. So, call and then call again if you need to. When you reach them, ask them all the questions you can think of; it will be hard to get hold of them again. And do ask for references.

Their references, usually other Bar Mitzvah mothers or mothers of brides, can enlighten you on such crucial factors as whether the musicians were prompt, took a lot of breaks, remembered to wear appropriate costumes, were too loud or too soft. (We already know this last is a matter of opinion, so judge your source carefully!)

Keep in mind that there may be some limits on the kind of music you can have in a particular setting. At your home, you will probably prefer a soloist or duet who adds just the right, festive touch rather than a four-piece combo whose members are crunched, sweating, in the corner. Some temples want only Israeli and folk dancing if your party is on Shabbat. Some don't allow electrified music on Shabbat. Some places don't have the wiring for amplification.

Though I would disagree with my friend Steve about what kind of music is "great," I do think that music is basic to your celebration. That doesn't mean you have to pay a fortune for Ricky Ricardo and his sixteen-piece Cha-Cha Band. I have seen one peppy accordionist get a whole large roomful of people dancing. A harpist who plays a great range of music is intriguing and sets a lovely mood. A singing guitarist is a popular and pleasant choice.

Nowhere is it written that you must have paid performers. How about your family? Is there a musician somewhere there who would love to have an audience (and deserves one)? My friend Susan ran a very snazzy cocktail party at the Museum of Fine Arts as a benefit for a hospital. Her college student niece played one of the museum's pianos beneath the medieval tapestries; it was all terribly elegant, and the music cost $50.

Whatever kind of music you arrange for, if you have room to dance, allow for the possibility of some Israeli circle dancing. Whether or not this is part of your background, there are many important advantages to this kind of dancing on this occasion. First, you don't need a partner. So widowed Aunt Tillie, your husband's newly separated colleague, the seven-year-old sister of the Bar Mitzvah, and all the thirteen-year-old girls with their beautiful new dresses can dance without being asked. Nobody has to be left out. The thirteen-year-old boys are unlikely to dance unless you bribe them, so don't worry about them. They will be watching the girls quite carefully. They might even join a circle dance, since they won't have to do anything gross and terrifying, like asking a girl to dance.

Another wonderful virtue of circle dancing is that you don't need to know any steps. And take it from the most awkward person who ever attended Joe Cornell's Dance Studio (where all the Jewish kids in northwest Detroit were sent in 1955) that when you don't have to know any steps, dancing is a lot more fun.

Even the shyest or oldest guest can stand at the edge of the circle and clap. It is a beautiful thing, especially when it's your occasion, to have everyone involved in the merrymaking.

One of the very nicest things about Israeli circle dances is that they are Jewish dances that Jews dance at Jewish celebrations. Talk about form following function. Even non-Jews are often delighted to join in, especially when they see how easy and joyful it is.

If you are extremely fortunate, you have a friend who will gather several other strong friends during the circle dancing and raise your son or daughter on a chair as a sign of honor and joy. This is a heady experience and may well be a unique one in the life of your child.

Now, about speeches by bandleaders, relatives, or anyone else: they give me the willies. I have actually heard some reasonably eloquent words from a parent or two. Mainly, however, speeches at Bar Mitzvahs are downright awful.

Most people are uncomfortable and unskilled at speaking to a crowd. If a relative or friend has something truly worthwhile to say to the Bar Mitzvah boy, it is likely to be something personal. This would probably be something that ought to be written in a note to the boy so he can save it, and so it doesn't need to suit any other audience but the right one.

True eloquence is hard to come by in famous after-dinner speakers, let alone one's relatives. Most people who get hold of the floor or, worse, the microphone get either tongue-tied or carried away.

If you feel you must have speakers, give each a strict time limit. I suggest, with all seriousness, a thirty-second limit. First, thirty seconds is actually a long time to speak; time it yourself. Second, the average adult has a continuous attention span of twenty-four seconds; they are always telling you that at teachers' conferences. And, finally, a wise and experienced rabbi once told me that the usual eulogy is only four minutes long—for a very famous person, maybe six. So much for long-winded speeches by thirteen-year-olds or about them.

By now you have detected my attitude toward speeches by Bar Mitzvah boys and family members. You will find that I am, if possible, less tolerant of speeches, announcements, and fanfare introductions by bandleaders. They don't know you from Adam, as my father used to say. Why on earth are you letting them announce your Aunt Hattie "all the way from Cincinnati," followed by the Ohio State fight song?

These announcements usually occur at a candlelighting ceremony where each of fourteen (one for good luck) candles is lit by some relative or close friend of the Bar Mitzvah family. I have been present at enough of these ceremonies to realize that they are not going to go away. They must fulfill some need, so I speculate on why they keep happening.

First, I think they probably stem from a desire by Bar Mitzvah parents to honor relatives and close friends and thank them for celebrating together. I am fully in favor of bestowing honors, but such honors ought to be accorded as aliyot at the synagogue services. Or you can have a series of toasts in a smaller group another time on the weekend, perhaps at a family party on Saturday night or Sunday at brunch. Then you can talk personally, and everyone will understand and appreciate it.

Another possible reason for these party ceremonies may be that we are all so influenced by television that we don't think something has really happened unless it has the appearance of a media event—a performance in front of a live audience, preferably videotaped. These reasons for a candlelighting ceremony are surely inappropriate and demean the occasion.

However, you can call on some special person to perform in a mode that is appropriate to the occasion. With advance warning, you can ask that the grace after meals (birkat hamazon) be led by your Bar Mitzvah, your husband, your rabbi, or a dear friend. You might even want to lead it yourself. Your Bar Mitzvah child will, of course, have led the kiddush over the wine and the motzi over the challah.

And the bandleader will have behaved best if he has performed only with his baton.

Navy raised printing ? OK.
Bandleader - NO speeches
return green hat

Chapter fourteen

Clothes make the man, but they make the woman crazy.

AT DINNER one night I mentioned that I had been downtown to look for a dress for Ben's Bar Mitzvah. (Ben was safely away at camp.) "Why is Ben going to wear a dress to his Bar Mitzvah?" asked Sam, who, at age seven, had more perspective about this event than I did at thirty-eight.

I would like to say that I got more reasonable about the central role of my dress for the Bar Mitzvah. I would like to say that, but it's not true; I only got worse. Four days before the Bar Mitzvah I decided I hated the dress I had already shortened. I whipped out immediately and got another. Later, of course, I returned it—though I'm still not sure about the first dress, the one I wore.

Obviously, the Bar Mitzvah boy himself is the central figure. However, boys are so utterly simple to suit up—not inexpensive, mind you, but straightforward. They don't have to decide what will be appropriate for the ceremony but also look festive at the celebration. They don't long for beautiful shoes with very high heels that are also utterly comfortable. They (usually) haven't been unsuccessful at losing the crucial ten pounds that would make them look so much younger. What Bar Mitzvah boy wants to look younger? Just be sure you don't get his suit too early; they grow suddenly and fast at this age.

Maybe somewhere there are women who are above all this, but I have never met a Bar Mitzvah mother who couldn't describe her dress in excruciating detail and maybe even some of the ones she returned.

What to wear rattles even sensible, self-knowledgeable mothers like Sharon, a psychiatric social worker with a busy private practice. She tried on her dress over and over for her husband Jerry's approval, but he only kept saying, "It's nice." She was waiting for him to say, "It's pretty." She wanted so much to look lovely, not just presentable.

I know that I was determined to avoid looking like my mother's generation of Bar Mitzvah mothers. They were all so girdled and rigid in their suits and hats. They all looked matronly and doubly uncomfortable because they dressed for the season that was about to begin. My mother, for instance, sweltered in a heavy woolen suit in September and froze in January in a linen dress and jacket of a verdant shade.

My husband perceived and expressed the true value of the Bar Mitzvah dress in an economic concept he referred to as CDPE: Cost of Dress Per Exposure. "You are justified," he explained, "in spending more than usual on this dress because it will have significantly more viewers than any other dress. Everybody you care about is going to see you in this dress so its cost per viewer cannot turn out to be high; it will be one of the most valuable dresses you will own. Not only that, but the dress will also be immortalized in photographs."

All of this brings to mind that expensive white satin and lace number with the veil that's been hanging in your basement all these years. But the Bar Mitzvah dress you can at least wear again, thereby again increasing its value.

Since you're going to be participating in a religious service and then receiving guests at a party, dress selection can get quite complicated. You can solve this by looking for a dress with a jacket or a suit with a fancy blouse. Or you can get a silk dress, like I did, and agonize about whether you'll be chilly or too fancy. Then you can end up, like I did, getting a velvet blazer, so as not to be too cold or too casual. (I turned out not to need the blazer that day but in the four years since I've worn out the elbows.)

Do call upon a close friend for help in this decision. Someone like my friend Susan is best. She has excellent judgment about clothes; she wears a lot of green, which makes her look especially good, and she never wears anything that makes her look ridiculous. She is honest; she arrives saying she's hungry and proceeds to eat two sandwiches. And she is willing to make house calls. This avoids the risk of getting rain on the dresses that might have to be returned.

There still will be moments when you are sure you got just the wrong thing. Elizabeth hated her shoes the week before. Miriam couldn't figure out what to do with the too-plain neckline of her dress, and Janice couldn't find a jacket to pull the whole thing together until the day before. The comforting thing is that, on the very day, you get too involved in the really important things, like remembering the day he was born, to give much of a thought to what you're wearing.

There are special issues, I am told, when the event is a Bat Mitzvah. Amy felt it was very important to let her daughter be the lovely one in the dress. The mother, she decided, ought not to steal the show, and so Amy wore a suit. Not every mother and daughter work it out this way, but it did seem to me a sensible and sensitive decision.

Now about hats. The last purely decorative hat I had worn was a mortarboard seventeen years earlier. Just trying on hats made me feel like Aunt Lillian. But I needed to cover my head, as you may be required to do at your synagogue. (Check it out with the rabbi in advance.)

I knew I could wear a kippah (yarmulka) or one of those lacy mantilla things. I didn't like the kippah idea (to me, they're for boys), and the mantilla reminded me too much of a bullfight. So I tried on all the hats I could find and hated them all. (You had to be Aunt Lillian to carry it off, I decided, or at least not wear glasses.)

I finally settled on making a feminine kippah from some antique lace my mother had hoped I'd use in my wedding gown. (I got married in the late sixties when brides weren't big on traditional frills.) The lacy kippah was sweet and quite small, but it counted.

Another nice solution to the hat problem was provided by a wonderful grandfather who did not spend his working life at a sewing machine for nothing. When his twin granddaughters became B'not Mitzvah, he piped a kippah for each with the fabric of her dress. Of course, he made one of the dresses, too, but not everybody is so fortunate in the grandfather department.

Whatever you do, make sure that your shoes are not brand new. Really old ones are best. And this goes for everyone in the family. This not only will make your outfits cheaper but will also make your whole day more comfortable.

Chapter fifteen

Family matters: More than ever

"MOTHER'S COMING" is a phrase that can produce great reassurance, I am told. For me, it always meant, "Now, are you ever going to get it." When your mother—and father, and aunts, uncles, grand-parents, and cousins, too—are coming, it is bound to produce strong emotions of one kind or the other. And the feelings will be just as powerful when any one of them is not coming—especially to your child's Bar or Bat Mitzvah.

The whole matter of family participation is fraught with your own emotional history multiplied by the anxiety of the event at hand. Then there is the variable of your spouse's family and their history and current tempests.

Many families provide support and reassurance for one another, and a Bar Mitzvah can bring out the best in them. My mother-in-law is the prime example. Since she is a devout Christian and the daughter of a missionary, it was hard for her (harder than I realized until I became a mother) when Van converted to Judaism. She was a gracious mother-of-the-groom at our wedding. Since then, she carefully and tactfully avoided involvement in most Jewish rituals, though the Chanukah gelt arrives promptly and with a perfect card.

However, she and my father-in-law are the only living grandparents, and Ben's Bar Mitzvah was approaching. A few months before the event she had the kindness and grace to say to us, "I don't know what Bar Mitzvah grandparents are supposed to do, but you just let us know and we'll do it." She offered specifically to advise about flowers and pay for them, since she is a devoted (and very talented) gardener.

She was also determined to fill the role of Bar Mitzvah grandmother at the ceremony and celebration, and did she ever! She and Van's Dad sat with us in the synagogue, looking proud, joyful, and beautiful. They stood for the blessing the family says. And they responded warmly to all congratulations, though she mildly chided those who didn't offer the proper "Mazel Tov" and instead said, "Congratulations." And when Ben was raised in a chair by a group of friends, she asked for and received the same honor for herself, this beautiful Bar Mitzvah grandmother. (She later worried unnecessarily that she shouldn't have done it.)

As your child veers nervously toward thirteen, you are likely to begin wondering whether certain family members are going to rise to the occasion or behave the way you dread they will. As my father used to reassure us, however, "Ninety percent of the things you worry about never happen." This is true, even for Bar Mitzvahs.

Karen was sure her aged grandmother from Palm Beach couldn't possibly make the trip to Hartford, but there she was, in the front row. Nina was resentful that Michael invited all his one hundred and twenty-five relatives and so few friends could be asked. But some relatives must have felt more remote than others because, a week before the Bat Mitzvah, Nina was able to telephone many friends and invite them, explaining that some of Michael's family couldn't come and she was delighted to be able to add friends she cared a lot about. Most of the friends came. And then there was Barbara's weird Uncle Harold, who would be out of place at anyone's table. He solved Barbara's problem (as he often does for family occasions) by just not showing up at all.

Moreover, there are some problems you can anticipate and solve in advance, especially if you gear up to ask for the help you will need. Abby was frantic because she felt obligated to have all the out-of-town relatives for dinner on Friday night and she had visions of herself incarcerated with twelve briskets for the week before. But because she is basically very sensible, she had the presence of mind to buy some of the menu already cooked and call upon the nearby relatives to help by bringing salad and dessert. Her sisters were all set to behave true to form and just come and be guests while she slaved, but Abby knew it was time to call in the debts that were owed her.

This is also the kind of occasion when a really good friend earns that label. Eighteen members of my husband's family replied with enthusiasm that they'd love to come to Ben's Bar Mitzvah. Most, of course, are Christian (two are Buddhist) and many had never been in a synagogue, let alone to a Bar Mitzvah. But my good friends made sure to seek them out for congratulations and conversation. Miriam even came over to meet my mother-in-law on Thanksgiving ten months before, "so, when we see each other at the Bar Mitzvah, we'll already be friends."

Some friends will anticipate your needs and some will need to be asked, but all willing help counts. In fact, according to Jewish tradition, you are doing something valuable in allowing another person to perform a mitzvah. Some exceedingly boring cousins present excellent opportunities for mitzvot.

You will need to call in the experts for some particularly sticky problems. Sarah was furious that her ex-husband Walter wanted the new wife to sit on the bimah with him and Sarah. Walter had been, at best, disinterested in their son's religious education. (At worst, he didn't pay for it and always dropped him off for Hebrew school at the wrong time.) Wisely, Sarah consulted the rabbi for advice well in advance of the Bar Mitzvah. Rabbis have more than a passing acquaintance with the wisdom of Solomon and the fallout from divorce. Sarah's rabbi, of course, allowed only the two natural parents to sit in the honored places.

If you have a special situation—a divorce or an intermarried family or a sibling who could use a special honor to assuage his jealousy or an aged uncle who needs to sit near the exit—speak to the rabbi about it. Judaism is thousands of years old, and so few problems can arise to which a rabbi hasn't ready access to a reasonable solution. Or he will likely be able to find one, now that he knows.

There are, however, problems that you can't head off. A great-aunt who always sulks and criticizes may act true to form on this occasion. Your brother, who has never been on time even to his wedding, will probably arrive after the Torah reading. Your two-year-old nephew will cling to his mother and demand a bottle as your daughter begins to chant the blessings. (Nobody encounters all of the preceding, but you are sure to get your share.)

A word here about grandparents of divorced spouses. Even if you are relieved and happy to be free of your former mate and you have arrived only with great difficulty at some working relationship for the Bar Mitzvah, go out of your way to be tolerant of the grandparents on the other side. It's their day, too, and they deserve some pleasure and pride in it.

It may be very difficult for you to teach this lesson to your children when there are bitter feelings all around. Yet you owe it to the kids to raise them to be polite and to appreciate the importance of their place in their own family history. If they need help with conversation, you can suggest they ask the grandparents about their own coming of age.

The rivalries and conflicts of a lifetime can't be quelled for this occasion. One young aunt of a Bar Mitzvah was successful, as she always had been, in diverting the family's attention to her. She found it imperative to take a bike ride near the motel just before her sister came to pick her up for Shabbat dinner with the family the night before the Bar Mitzvah. Since she got lost in the unfamiliar town, a search party had to be sent out, and the Shabbat dinner was late and cold. I think there is something to be said for letting such a relative stay lost.

Then there was the reborn marathoner uncle who always jogged in the afternoon and so missed the last hour of the party. And there was the always-huffy aunt who took umbrage at not being asked to light a candle (though her mate lit one). How many relatives does it take to light a candle? I think the aunt is still not speaking to the Bar Mitzvah parents and even the boy himself, who is thereby confirmed in his hunch that adulthood is not all it's cracked up to be.

Deaths and distance and unresolved hostility meant that I would be the only member of "my side" of the family at Ben's Bar Mitzvah. It also meant there would be no Jewish family. This could have been very sad, but good friends filled the place of missing family. And so Jane was there to chant her aliyah. She and I lived in an attic together during graduate school, plotting glamorous futures for ourselves. And through her WATS line at work in New York we were able to continue to reevaluate our plots, as husbands and children and jobs cramped or expanded our styles. Jane has actively fulfilled the role of Ben's godmother since he was born. She brought him exotic robes from Morocco when he was two and sent him Steve Martin records when I was still rather sure he was too young for them. Jane is pretty antireligious and not given to public performing, but she was more than willing to learn the blessings from a transliteration and tape Ben made for her. She got a snazzy suit and cape, brought husband and baby, and got here in time for Shabbat dinner with the family, which she is.

In addition, David, a dear friend from Van's law school days, has become, with his family, so close to us that our children used to ask if they were our cousins. So it was only right that David held the Torah, assisted by his daughter Kate, who had her dress two months in advance.

And all Van's relatives, as even our cateress commented, "did very well." I know that she meant they ate well for people with no previous Bar Mitzvah experience. But they also danced and laughed and celebrated "very well" too, to say nothing of their enthusiastic attendance at a two-and-a-half-hour service in a language foreign to them.

You probably don't need my alternately reassuring and horrifying stories to make you apprehensive and hopeful. But do always keep in mind the advice Helen gave me when I met her in the bookstore the week before the Bar Mitzvah. I regaled her with all my worries about the family issues that would come up. She listened very sympathetically and then reminded me that she, too, had a family (and three Bat Mitzvahs behind her). In fact, she ventured to assert, "Everybody has a family. Even all your guests. I think they'll understand."

Chapter sixteen

What will we do with them? The out-of-towners

HOWIE IS THE ONLY grown person I know who is able to say, "My whole family lives in the same zip code." And he doesn't just mean that he still lives with his wife and their two children. He means the whole mishpoche—his parents, grandparents, two brothers, and two sisters (all married)—live in 02159.

Most of us have many more zip codes to deal with. But we have to figure out how to get them all reasonably settled in the Bar Mitzvah zip code for one weekend. As they say in *Fiddler on the Roof*, "It isn't easy."

Uncle Harry, as everyone knows, is highly allergic. Though he will bring his own pillow and his can of dust remover, he is going to need a very clean, austere place. Jenny and David will need a room with a crib, somewhere near a drugstore, since they never remember to bring disposable diapers. And they'll need a very competent sitter for someplace less confining than the motel room for the whole morning and afternoon Saturday. Cousin Marge, the most beloved of all, is making a very expensive trip here from Duluth and so you'll have to find a friend who can put her up and walk with her to the services (since Marge is Orthodox), and, by the way, she's bringing her daughter and grandson.

Unless you've got relatives who will stay only with the queen at the Helmsley Hotel and can foot the bill, scout around for two possible guest accommodations. One should be a reasonably priced motel which has basic clean rooms and charges accordingly. The other should be the spare room of some kind friends, who know what it is to have houseguests and are willing, anyway.

Make those motel reservations very early and for the maximum rooms you'll need. (I did it six months in advance.) You won't have to put up any money far in advance. Don't forget to find out about cribs and cots.

Miss Manners and Emily herself agree that out-of-town guests should reasonably be expected to pay for themselves. (They discuss only weddings, but I generalize.) So, after Aunt Tillie's enthusiastic response note has arrived, write to tell her that you're delighted she can come and that you've made reservations at the Last Resort Motel, 123 O'Leary Street, in Peoria Heights, and a $34 deposit is needed a week in advance.

The friends with the available spare room should receive the very nicest plant or flowers from the party. If you happen to have an extra bottle of champagne left, that's a nice touch. You should also sincerely offer in reciprocity to keep their Aunt Tillie when she comes to town for the wedding, Bar Mitzvah, or graduation.

You may have noticed that I did not suggest that you have any houseguests yourself. That was not an oversight. A nervous Bar Mitzvah family (even a calm one) does not need anyone else living with them. Even the most considerate of mothers or cousins will need to shower, find a safety pin, or eat breakfast. You just don't need anyone else to worry about. Let them scare up their own hot water, safety pins, and English muffins.

However, you are likely to feel (rightly) that you might offer a bit more in the way of gatherings for these nice people who have come some distance to share your celebration. Lest you think with dismay this is becoming some kind of college football weekend, consider that Aunt Grace has come all the way from Tucson and that she hasn't seen you or the rest of the family in six years. You yourself might also enjoy the chance to chat in a more leisurely way with some of the out-of-towners either before or after the ceremony and larger party. I suggest a Friday night dinner (or better, just dessert), a Saturday night sandwich supper, or a Sunday brunch. If you are a nut like me, you can have all three.

I didn't want to be fixing dinner for thirty-five on Friday, and I don't have a sister to do it. So I invited people coming in town that evening to stop by for dessert (paper plates) if they could come by 9 p.m. At 10:30 we asked them all to leave. Since there's a lot of festivity in the air by Friday night, you'll probably feel like beginning the celebration then. This also gives you a chance to hug a dear, old roommate or cousin you'd otherwise see first under more formal circumstances at the service.

The leftovers from the big party on Saturday can provide most of the food for Saturday night's supper. Our family couldn't have eaten them in a week by ourselves, but they were the perfect light supper for the family and friends who stopped by. If you can't get the leftovers or don't want to serve them, you might get a deli tray.

Whatever you do, make it as easy as possible on yourself. Paper plates and cups and plastic utensils are a must. So is a helping person. We hired a college student. We should have hired two. Let your friends help you, too. Most everyone loves to help for a simcha. I have a fond memory of Sharon and Rebecca, two of my college roommates, taking charge of the cake-cutting in the midst of a sea of people in my kitchen.

Some family and friends will leave by Sunday morning. Some will take the opportunity to sleep late or visit the local botanical gardens, science museum, or video arcade. But there will still be others, like the grandparents and a few close friends, who will be around. You don't need to have any kind of grand event, but if you have bagels and cream cheese, orange juice, and coffee, you'll give them and yourself another opportunity to be together. If this sounds like altogether too much togetherness, do follow your instincts. But if it appeals, do it. There's so much trouble in the world and not nearly enough opportunities to celebrate, especially with the people you care about.

These surrounding events also give you a chance to invite the young or distantly related children you didn't want to invite to the service or reception. Your cousins will be pleased to show off their kids to everyone; in your house, they'll be able to mind them in less restrictive circumstances than at the temple.

Since you have correctly perceived by now that I am some kind of Bar Mitzvah addict, you will not be surprised to discover that I sent Uncle Fred and the cousins off to their eight-hour train ride with a picnic lunch (more leftovers) and an extra bottle of champagne. Amtrak never had it so good.

Before we pack the relatives off, a word about their close-range traveling—which is to say, just because you could put the car on automatic carpool and it would find the temple by itself doesn't mean that the relatives can. Your town will be confusing to any out-of-towners and they'll need help. I always remember the French Canadian in Quebec who gave us directions in English. "You can't help missing it," he encouraged us, and we couldn't.

You could just get the out-of-towners a map of the area, but it is also useful to write out directions to the different places they'll have to find. Your Aunt Ellen, eight hundred miles from home and driving a rented car, already overslept because of the time change. She shouldn't have to miss the haftarah.

It may really humble you (as it did us) to learn exactly how confusing your city is when you try to write out directions. You can accomplish this best by driving the routes yourself. We put one hundred and eighty miles on the car figuring out the three-mile circuit from motel to temple to our house. But we didn't lose anyone.

Chapter seventeen

Which are the jonquils and which are the truffles? Flowers, table groupings, and other trivial pursuits

IF I HAD ONLY MYSELF to please, I would have ordered a great supply of my favorite miniature candy bars. But, for a Bar Mitzvah party, only pretty chocolates and fancy nuts would do. They were as basic as flowers and a hat.

I had been told the name of the appropriate candy establishment. This was going to be a cinch, especially after figuring out the menu and how to juggle the bills.

So, a few days before the Bar Mitzvah, I found my way into this small charming shoppe, a vision right out of Hansel and Gretel. I just stood around sniffing contentedly for a while, until the proprietress stepped out of the kitchen to greet me. It was easy to tally up the order, since the cateress had given me the formula per table "and less for the kids' table, since they just throw it at each other."

After I put in the order I said I'd pick it up on Thursday. "This coming Thursday?" The candymaker was in a huff at my outrageous short notice. For once I remembered not to apologize and instead concentrated on getting the job done. I just asked, "Can't you have it ready on Thursday?" And, albeit reluctantly, it turned out she could.

There are librarians who just love to tell you that the book can't be taken out and receptionists who rejoice that the doctor couldn't possibly see you until 1990. You are sure to run into some of their ilk as you assemble the elements for your celebration. One rule will help you keep your perspective and stay on track and get the job done. It will also help you avoid inflicting serious bodily injury on manipulative tradespeople.

The rule is: don't apologize. A businesslike, straightforward attitude can help you cut through the layers of emotional parlaying that many caterers, florists, and hairdressers like to use to make sure you know they're important. You already know. That's why you called them. Now just get on with it. You're important, too.

Especially don't apologize for your ignorance of their field. Your specialty so far has been social work or litigation or oriental rugs. You have certainly been able to master the intricacies of diplomatic carpooling. There's no reason you can't easily comprehend the range of floral possibilities or wine choices. It's the florist's job to teach you to tell the amaryllis from the jonquils and whether either of them blooms in May and at what cost.

Once you've been acquainted with the choices, you will find that your own taste and financial limits will lead you fairly easily to a reasonable selection.

My childhood experience convinced me that you couldn't be Jewish and garden. Oh, sure, there were kibbutzniks, but they just raised practical, venerable things like olive trees and figs. (Actually, Israel is an important exporter of beautiful, reasonably priced flowers to the United States and Europe, but I kept remembering

Tu B'Shvat celebrations in 1953.) A few years ago I began tentatively venturing out into the alien territory of the backyard to put in some indestructible impatiens, but I still felt hopelessly inadequate to select flowers for a state occasion.

I was more dismayed when the florist showed me endless photographs of different Bar Mitzvah bowers. Upon closer scrutiny, the choice got easier, though. Most of the flowers were too tall, too massive, too impermanent, and too expensive.

Tall flowers had kept me from talking to guests across the table at previous Bar Mitzvah parties (after the hostess must have gone nuts arranging the table groupings).

Heaping arrays of flowers are less lovely than a few selected blossoms. This I learned from my mother-in-law, the gardener. She always says (quite rightly; try it yourself), "When you're done arranging the flowers, take out half."

Cut flowers don't last, but plants do and can be given to important guests. (One especially thoughtful Bat Mitzvah delivered all her plants to a nursing home.) And all these prohibitions conspire to help keep down the cost of the flowers.

So it turned out to be pretty easy for me, a person who didn't even own gardening gloves, to order one white mum plant for each table. It will sort itself out for you, too.

Do remain flexible about the flowers, however, because cost and availability are chancy. The weather turned cold early and so the mums we ordered came in costing twice as much as planned. After a flurry of phone calls, I canceled the mums and drove out in the country for pumpkins instead. A pumpkin, surrounded by autumn leaves (buy them, don't pick them), looked jolly and festive on each table that October day.

I did end up getting a few plants to jazz up the buffet table and our house, but I just selected those at the neighborhood florist on the basis of what looked pretty and was reasonably priced. In the midst of a busy week it was nice to spend a quiet hour wandering around in the greenhouse. No one went into ecstasies over the flowers or the pumpkins, but the guests to whom I gave them seemed pleased.

Flowers, plants, or even pumpkins are not the only choices. A colleague of mine with really fine values eschewed table ornaments entirely. Instead, on the center of each table was a scroll from the Jewish National Fund. In lieu of flowers, it said, five trees had been planted in Israel in honor of the Bar Mitzvah of Seth.

Now about those tables. Even as you make up the guest list, you'll probably begin to ponder: whom can we put with Cousin Helen? She's too (select one or more) intelligent, dumb, opinionated, shy, rude, gentle for everyone we know.

Where to seat the guests is the kind of issue a person like me really grooves on, and I can (and did) make quite a career of it. With my strong interest in matchmaking (marriages and friendships), my equally strong aversion for making anybody unhappy, and my great indecision, I prolonged this job to the very morning of Ben's Bar Mitzvah.

I had a little slip of paper with each guest's name on it so I could set up a model of the seating groups on my dining room table. For weeks before the event I was fascinated by organizing and reorganizing them into all kinds of clever groups. I was teaching school at the time and quite busy but never too tired to have another go at rearranging the little pieces of paper.

I tried not to involve my husband too often in what was bound to be an endless task. However, I just couldn't resist wanting him to applaud my great sociological discoveries. More than once, I asked him to drag himself out of bed late at night because I had just made a brilliant arrangement. See, both these women used the same obstetrician! Look, this is perfect: both these couples supported McGovern in 1972. Isn't this great: they all have at least one parent who is a psychiatrist.

While I did enjoy my time in the role of *Hello, Dolly*, there really is a better, simpler way of arranging groups. Diane hit upon it. She had had my same looney fascination with organizing guests. She spent the semester before her wedding arranging model tables in her notebook during "Europe, 1848–1914" lectures. She had probably put in more time than I had. Finally it dawned upon her that there was only one rule to follow: seat each guest with someone he knows, if at all possible.

After all, she reminded me, don't you feel glad (even relieved) to find people you know at a party? How much time is there in this busy life to have fun with your friends? A Bar Mitzvah is a perfect opportunity to do that. Don't make it into a therapeutic encounter group or a strained conversation among strangers.

Now that everyone is seated, what about photographs? First, I suggest you find out whether your temple allows picture-taking on Shabbat. If it does, you should ponder very carefully what you want of the pictures and the photographer.

You'll want to avoid making this Bar Mitzvah ceremony into one long photo-opportunity. It's nice to record your family at this great juncture in their lives, and this is a good chance to take pictures of all the relatives. They probably are rarely assembled in such numbers. However, you will remember this day; you don't need to be able to reenact it in living color. Why get stuck owning (and paying for) a picture of every guest with napkins on laps in a smiling semicircle around half-eaten food?

If you must have pictures at the ceremony and celebration, make sure your photographer is selective and unobtrusive. Better yet, take pictures at home before you leave for the synagogue and at a smaller gathering of relatives the next day. Then you can just experience the Bar Miizvah instead of staging it.

While you're over at the temple checking out the rules on photographs and making sure the curtains don't clash with the napkins, take some time to make the acquaintance of the temple custodian. Learn his name and don't forget it after the Bar Mitzvah. This very important person knows every caterer in town, where to find all the extra chairs, and how to turn up the air conditioning. He's had lots of experience dealing with ruffled party-givers, and he ought to be appreciated for all his knowledge, his calmness, and his hard work. Remember that he, like all workers who are purposely underpaid, should receive a reasonable check in anticipation of his effort, attention, and kindness on the big day. You may prefer to give it afterwards. But I wanted this nice man to know that I was both generous and confident in him, and so I gave it beforehand.

What with all these trips to the temple, the florist, and the candy store, you probably won't be home much in the last week or so before the Bar Mitzvah. That is probably just as well because the painters are there.

That is, if you're like most Bar Mitzvah mothers I know, you've decided that you've just got to paint the living room, retile the bathroom, get curtains for the den, or paper the hallway before the Bar Mitzvah. You've lived with these imperfections for years, but, suddenly, they seem unacceptable.

It's inevitable that you feel freshly self-conscious about your home as you imagine the army of relatives marching in. The fixing up seems to be an unavoidable part of the event, a magnified version of picking the right dress. Probably Aunt Hilda won't even notice the new wallpaper, but you'll feel better in case she does. And you'll get to enjoy that nice colorful design for years.

The only thing I can suggest to make this decorating project less of a hassle is to schedule it all to be done months before the event. Then, when the painter is late, as he always is, you probably won't still have ladders in the hall when the guests arrive.

Chapter eighteen

How do you spell "sincerely"? Thank-yous and their gifts

WHEN RICHARD BECAME Bar Mitzvah in 1938, his parents took the whole family to lunch at the neighborhood delicatessen, an extravagant affair for those depression days when the family sometimes couldn't afford to eat at home. The rich uncle gave Richard his only gift: twenty-five dollars, a magnificent sum equal to the cost of the celebration. If ever there was an appropriate gift, that was it.

In these days of considerably greater affluence, selecting an appropriate and desirable gift, not just affording a gift, has become the problem. Several of our guests actually called to ask what Ben might want. In case you receive such a call, you would do well to suggest a large category, like books, from which the giver may make an economically appropriate choice. Another possibility is to say, "I know Debbie is eager to have a computer. Perhaps you could contribute to her computer fund."

Such replies are polite. They leave the cost of the gift up to the buyer, and yet give him some sense of what would be appropriate. It would be wrong just to be evasive, but it is never polite to ask for a specific gift.

You yourself may be looking for guidance about gifts on the occasion of so many Bar and Bat Mitzvah celebrations. For, if you are in the throes of preparing for one, it is likely your friend Harriet's boy is scheduled for the next week and Cousin Don's daughter in Buffalo will be Bat Mitzvah in November. So, perhaps, it's time you considered the matter of Bar and Bat Mitzvah gifts first from the other side, just to smooth out the process for yourself.

On this occasion, money is often given instead of something more permanent. Partly it's because many guests don't really know the child, but mostly it's because thirteen is such a transitional age. If you select a gift of permanent value (a reference book or a classic piece of jewelry), it may be disappointing to the recipient at the time he receives it. However, if you give him something he desperately wants now, he may find it tiresome in just a few months.

So you can give him money (in cash, check, or bond), and then he can spend it on something he very much wants now (which changes week to week) or put it toward something major, like a computer or stereo he'll save to get later on. He can always put it in the college fund. And some share of the cash gifts ought to be set aside for Tzedakah. He could always volunteer to help pay for the reception, but that probably hasn't been done since 1938.

Books are excellent presents, particularly reference books. You'll just have to accept that they won't seem thrilling now. However, they are bound to come in handy down the line. If you're sure the Bar Mitzvah boy already has a dictionary and you also happen to be very fond of him and you have a significant amount of money to spend, you might consider an unabridged dictionary.

Our son was quite impressed when one arrived; it was his heaviest gift and it inspired him to investigate whether there was any word he could think of that wasn't in it.

Other gift books to consider include:

New Oxford Book of American Verse

Oxford Companion to American History

Complete works of Emily Dickinson, Robert Frost, or Carl Sandburg

An atlas (they range from grand to very usable; they can cover the United States, the world, Israel, or history)

Heritage, by Abba Eban

My People, by Abba Eban

A Treasury of Jewish Humor, edited by Nathan Ausubel

The Jewish Catalog, edited by Richard Siegel and Sharon and Michael Strassfeld

The Big Book of Jewish Humor, edited and annotated by William Novak and Moshe Woldoks

I could suggest that you give *Bartlett's Familiar Quotations*, but then what would I give?

Other attractive gifts include: a fine globe, a calculator, computer software, a magazine subscription (e.g., *National Geographic* or *Science*), jewelry, a jewelry case, a shofar, a Havdalah set, a silk scarf, a pen and pencil set, a backpack, leather gloves, a wallet, or a traveling kit.

A most interesting and unusual gift is a reproduction of the front page of *The New York Times* for the day of the Bar Mitzvah's birth. You can order one from University Microfilms (1-800-521-0600).

Sometimes you're not invited to a Bar Mitzvah because your friendship with the family wouldn't warrant it, or they're having a very small celebration. If you feel very warmly toward the child or the family and you'd like to, it is perfectly lovely to send a small gift. I know how pleased I was when a dear friend's mother sent a charming note and a small check. It is also quite appropriate to send just the congratulatory note. It is always nice to share the good wishes by making a donation to a charity in honor of a Bar or Bat Mitzvah.

The gifts are likely to be a real highlight of the occasion for the new Jewish adult. Not so the thank-you notes. But short, well-written, prompt, perfectly spelled, even occasionally charming thank-you notes are another key element in this rite of passage from child to adult.

There should, first of all, be a careful record kept of all gifts and their donors. You will probably need to help set up this list, but it should gradually become the responsibility of the Bar Mitzvah himself. (You must check on it from time to time; this is, after all, just the beginning of maturity.) I suggest you use the card file already assembled for the invitations, described in chapter twelve. Then all the information needed to complete the thank-you note is in one place. Your note-writer shouldn't have to scream down to the kitchen, "Hey, Mom, what do I call the Cohens? Do you call a vet 'doctor'?" Make it easy for him or her to act independently.

However independent he is, you will need to assist him at several stages of the process. You'll need to help him select the informal notes he will have on hand for his thank-you notes. You can use plain, small, folded, white notes, or you can have them printed with his initials or name. Don't pick the notes that have "Thank you" already emblazoned on them. This is to be a personal expression of gratitude, not a printout. Your son or daughter will have his or her own ideas about colors and style, but I suggest you respectfully steer your youngster in the direction of simplicity. The ones that are decorated to look like flowery curtains, though they may be popular this year, may well look grotesque by the time she's writing thank-you notes for next Chanukah's check from Grandma. And be sure to get plenty of this stationery; there are bound to be mistakes which will require a second copy.

Now for the substance of the notes. You will need to give some lessons and to review at least the first notes. Assure your Bar or Bat Mitzvah that a note of thanks need not be long, but it must mention the specific gift in a grateful way, and it must be prompt. If your child sincerely does want to add a line about his pleasure at having the donor present at his Bar Mitzvah, that is a nice touch. Just don't make it a formula.

This is a good time for your child to become acquainted with a book on etiquette. *Emily Post* and *Miss Manners' Guide to Excruciatingly Correct Behavior,* as well as many other etiquette books, give fine samples of thank-you notes. In the course of this exposure to an etiquette book, your Bar Mitzvah may notice how much other useful advice for important occasions is found there. It's not all lists of which spoon to use first when you dine with the king.

Thanking someone for money is not really different from thanking him for anything else. The recipient needs to be specific in this case, too; he should mention specifically how he plans to use the money. He may mention the amount or he may simply write "your (very) generous gift." (The "very" is used for whatever you consider a remarkably bountiful amount.) Be careful how the thank-you for money is phrased. Ruth found that her son was writing thank-you notes for money that sounded more like receipts.

Spelling counts in such notes, as in all writing. It shows that the writer means to be taken seriously. You will probably need to supervise.

Here are some examples that might help your young friend, in case both Emily and Miss Manners are out of the library:

Dear Uncle Jim,

I am so grateful for your generous gift of $50 which has gone directly into my stereo fund. Maybe when I get my stereo, I'll be able to teach you to break-dance!

It was wonderful that you could come all the way from Akron for my Bar Mitzvah.

Love,

Josh

Dear Mr. and Mrs. Cohen,

I am very pleased to have my own thesaurus. I know I'll be using it a lot in English Comp this fall.

Thank you!

Sincerely,

Rebecca

Please note that the messages are short and simple and written in conversational English. A long-winded, pompous note is much less genuine. Sincerity is what you're after.

And speaking of sincere thanks, you yourself may be feeling quite grateful after the Bar Mitzvah that the Hebrew teacher was so patient, that the caterer was consistently calm in the face of your hysteria, or that the rabbi made your father-in-law feel so welcome and important. It's a very nice time for you to write some notes of your own. You can borrow a snappy new pen from your son or daughter.

Appendix

I. Help for Special Needs Bar Mitzvahs

  A. National Organizations

       Jewish Braille Institute of America, Inc.
       110 East 30th Street
       New York, NY 10016
       (212) 889-2525

       P'TACH (Parents for Torah for All Children)
       62 Green Street
       Brookline, MA 02146

       Union of American Hebrew Congregations
       (Reform Union)
       838 Fifth Avenue
       New York, NY 10021
       (212) 249-0100

       Union of Orthodox Jewish Congregations of America
       45 West 36th Street
       New York, NY 10018
       (212) 563-4000

       United Synagogue of America
       (Conservative Union)

155 Fifth Avenue
New York, NY 10010
(212) 533-7800

B. Jewish Education Boards and Bureaus (most have a special needs consultant)

Bureau of Jewish Education
1745 Peachtree Street, N.W.
Atlanta, GA 30309
(404) 873-1248

Bureau of Jewish Education (Boston)
333 Nahanton Street
Newton Centre, MA 02159
(617) 965-7350

Board of Jewish Education
618 South Michigan Avenue
Chicago, IL 60605
(312) 427-5570

Bureau of Jewish Education
6505 Wilshire
Los Angeles, CA 90048
(213) 852-1234

Board of Jewish Education
426 West 58th Street
New York, NY 10019
(212) 245-8200

Board of Jewish Education (Washington, D.C.)
9325 Brookville Road
Silver Spring, MD 20910
(301) 589-3180

C. Boston Area Temples and Jewish Schools Providing Special Education Programs as of January, 1985 (list compiled by Dr. Sandy Miller-Jacobs, Special Needs Coordinator, Bureau of Jewish Education in Boston)

Boston (02215)
   Temple Israel
   Longwood Avenue & Plymouth Street
   (617) 566-3960
   Principal: Rabbi Ronne Friedman
   Contact: Marlene Moskowitz

Brockton (02401)
   Temple Beth Emunah
   Torrey & Pearl Streets
   Principal: Rhoda Factor
   Contact: Dorothy Belman

Brookline (02146)
   Maimonides Day School
   Philbrick Road
   (617) 232-4414
   Principal: Rabbi David Shapiro
   Contact: Phyllis Fleishman

Lexington (02173) (Joint program called "B'Yahad")
   Temple Emunah
   9 Piper Road
   (617) 861-0303
   Principal: Carolyn Keller
   Contact: Marcie Greenfield

   Temple Isaiah
   55 Lincoln Street
   (617) 862-7160
   Principal: Lois Edelstein

Malden (02148)
  Temple Tifereth Israel
  539 Salem Street
  Principal: Jack Sparks

Natick (01760)
  Temple Israel
  145 Harford Avenue
  (617) 653-8640
  Principal: David Ginsburg

Newton (02159)
  Temple Emanuel
  385 Ward Street
  (617) 332-5770
  Principal: Dr. Trudy Karger
  Contact: Florence Ziffer

  Simcha Program at High School of Jewish Studies
  % Schechter Day School
  Shoolman Campus
  130 Wheeler Road
  (617) 332-4722
  Contact: Emily Lipoff

Randolph (02368)
  Temple Beth Am
  871 North Main Street
  (617) 963-6836
  Principal: Terri Swartz Russell

Sharon (02067)
  Temple Sinai
  100 Ames Street
  (617) 828-8587
  Principal: Martha Aft

Swampscott (01970)
    Ye'He Or
    % Temple Beth El
    55 Atlantic Avenue
    (617) 599-8005
    Principal: Mark Casso

Westwood (02090)
    Beth David of Westwood
    P. O. Box 458
    Principal: Cara Zubren

D. Jewish Camping for Special Needs Children

Tikvah Program
Camp Ramah in New England
1330 Beacon Street
Brookline, MA 02146
(617) 232-7400

E. Helpful Books for Parents

Hammer, Reuven. *The Other Child in Jewish Education, A Handbook on Learning Disabilities.* New York. United Synagogue Commission on Jewish Education, 1979.

Strassfeld, Sharon, and Strassfeld, Michael, eds. *The Second Jewish Catalog with the Jewish Yellow Pages.* Philadelphia: Jewish Publication Society, 1976.

II. For "twinning" with a Soviet Jewish Bar or Bat Mitzvah

Council for Soviet Jews
1411 K Street NW
Washington, DC 20005
(202) 393-4117

III. Invitations

    A. Below is the invitation for our son Ben's Bar Mitzvah:

Van and Alice Lanckton

cordially invite you to worship with them

at the Bar Mitzvah of their son

Benjamin Edward

Saturday, the twenty-fourth of October

at half after nine o'clock

Temple Emanuel

385 Ward Street

Newton Centre, Massachusetts

Luncheon following service   Please reply

B. Here are samples of Crane and Co. Bar and Bat Mitzvah invitations, which are available only through authorized Crane retail stationers:

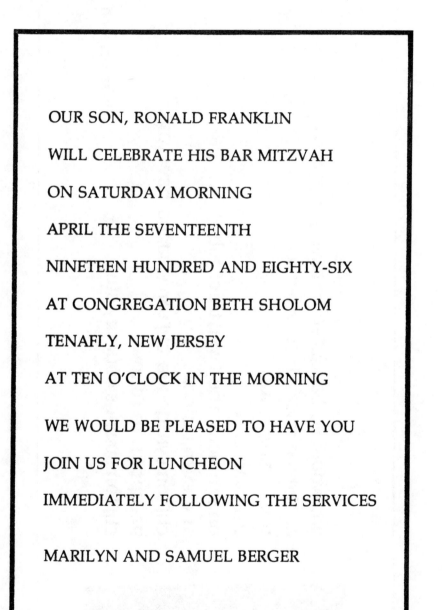

OUR SON, RONALD FRANKLIN

WILL CELEBRATE HIS BAR MITZVAH

ON SATURDAY MORNING

APRIL THE SEVENTEENTH

NINETEEN HUNDRED AND EIGHTY-SIX

AT CONGREGATION BETH SHOLOM

TENAFLY, NEW JERSEY

AT TEN O'CLOCK IN THE MORNING

WE WOULD BE PLEASED TO HAVE YOU

JOIN US FOR LUNCHEON

IMMEDIATELY FOLLOWING THE SERVICES

MARILYN AND SAMUEL BERGER

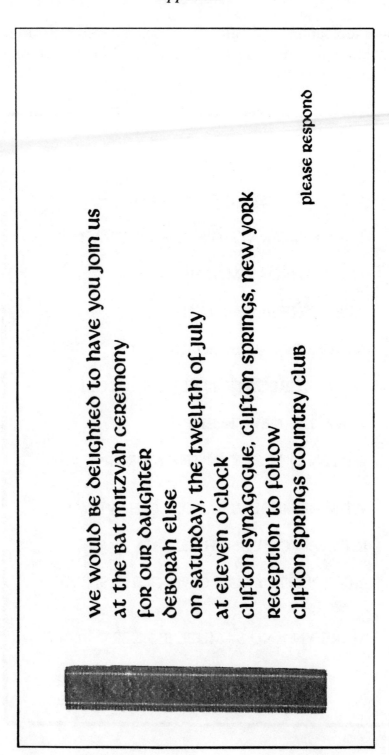

we would be delighted to have you join us

at the bat mitzvah ceremony

for our daughter

deborah elise

on saturday, the twelfth of july

at eleven o'clock

clifton synagogue, clifton springs, new york

reception to follow

clifton springs country club

please respond

C. This invitation for a friend's Bat Mitzvah was done by
   Sharon Savitsky of Brooklyn, New York:

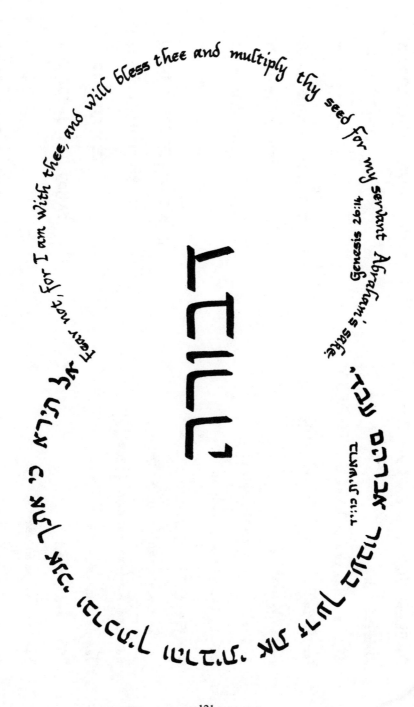

בס״ד

בשבת פרשת קודש תולדות בתנו

ונתן לירקה

בתורה כבת

מצוה לעצמה ולמען סרבנית

העליה מברית המועצות

קירה וולבובסקי

אסיר ציון בבריה״מ

בכבוד רב נבקש מכם להצטרף

ונשמח לשמוע שמחתנו

מיום ????

On Shabbat Toldot our daughter

Deborah Joy

will be called to the Torah as a Bat Mitzvah

For herself and for Soviet refusenik

Kira Volvolsky

It would give us great pleasure

to have you worship with us

and join us for luncheon

on the twenty-eighth of November

nineteen hundred and eighty-one

Temple Emanuel

385 Ward Street

Newton, Massachusetts

Marsha and Marc Slotnick

Kindly Reply

D. Printed invitations which include the Soviet "twin" are available now from many sources, including:

Arthur Chase
Chase Paper Co.
Oak Street
Westboro, MA 01581
(617) 754-6801

IV. Books on Judaism for Parents

Donin, Hayim Halevy. *To Be a Jew*. New York: Basic Books, 1972.

Kushner, Harold S. *When Children Ask About God*. New York: Schocken Books, 1976.

Kushner, Harold S. *When Bad Things Happen to Good People*. New York: Schocken Books, 1981.

Siegel, Richard; Strassfeld, Michael; and Strassfeld, Sharon, eds. *The Jewish Catalog*. Philadelphia: Jewish Publication Society, 1973.

Strassfeld, Sharon, and Strassfeld, Michael, eds. *The Second Jewish Catalog with the Jewish Yellow Pages*. Philadelphia: Jewish Publication Society, 1976.

Strassfeld, Sharon, and Strassfeld, Michael, eds. *The Third Jewish Catalog*. Philadelphia: Jewish Publication Society, 1980.

Bibliography

BRIDGER, David, and Wolk, Samuel, eds. *The New Jewish Encyclopedia*. New York: Behrman House, 1976.

EISENBERG, Azriel, ed. *Eyewitnesses to American Jewish History, Part 4: The American Jew 1915–1969*. New York: Union of American Hebrew Congregations, 1982.

HAMMER, Reuven. *The Other Child in Jewish Education, A Handbook on Learning Disabilities*. New York: United Synagogue Commission on Jewish Education, 1979.

KATSH, Abraham, ed. *Bar Mitzvah*. New York: Shengold Publishers, Inc., 1976.

MARTIN, Judith. *Miss Manners' Guide to Excruciatingly Correct Behavior*. New York: Warner Books, Inc., 1982.

POST, Elizabeth P. *The New Emily Post's Etiquette*. New York: Thomas Y. Crowell, 1975.

SIEGEL, Richard; Strassfeld, Michael; and Strassfeld, Sharon, eds. *The Jewish Catalog*. Philadelphia: Jewish Publication Society, 1973.

STRASSFELD, Sharon, and Strassfeld, Michael, eds. *The Second Jewish Catalog with the Jewish Yellow Pages*. Philadelphia: Jewish Publication Society, 1976.